Women's Ordination and the San Antonio Compromise

Michael G. Coleman, D. Min, Ph.D.

TEACH Services, Inc.
PUBLISHING
www.TEACHServices.com • (800) 367-1844

Copyright © 2021 Michael G. Coleman
Copyright © 2021 TEACH Services, Inc.
ISBN-13: 978-1-4796-1301-4 (Paperback)
ISBN-13: 978-1-4796-1302-1 (ePub)
Library of Congress Control Number: 2021902514

All Bible text references are taken from the New King James Version of the Bible unless
otherwise stated. Public domain.

Bible references labeled (NIV) are taken from the Holy Bible, New International
Version®, NIV® Copyright ©1973, 1978, 1984, 2011 by Biblica, Inc.® Used by permis-
sion. All rights reserved worldwide.

Published by

TEACH Services, Inc.
P U B L I S H I N G
www.TEACHServices.com • (800) 367-1844

Table of Contents

Introduction

Why write a book on women's ordination—especially after all the studies that have been presented by the Theology of Ordination Study Committee (TOSC), the Biblical Research Committees (BRCs), and various authors? There are other issues that seem to be more pivotal to the health and mission of the Seventh-day Adventist Church than the question of whether or not women should be ordained as pastors, so why spend more time discussing and explicating this topic?

First of all, in spite of the rejection of women's ordination in the 2015 San Antonio General Conference Session, the Seventh-day Adventist denomination is still very divided on the issue. In view of our lack of cohesion on this issue, the average church member is looking for a user-friendly resource to help them understand what the Bible teaches on this subject. In response to this need, the present book provides biblically based answers to important questions on women's ordination in a clear and simple format.

Second, the women's ordination debate has exposed some closely related issues of paramount importance to the unity and viability of the Seventh-day Adventist Church. For example, almost in tandem with other Protestant churches that have either endorsed women's ordination or have given mixed signals concerning it, there is a growing attitude of accommodation toward homosexuality and the LGBT community in the Seventh-day Adventist Church. At the same time, the authority of the Bible is being undermined by an increasing tendency among many Adventists to assert that certain passages of Scripture, which do not support their ideological viewpoint, are culturally conditioned. The issues surrounding the authority of the Bible and proper methods of interpretation are the most crucial of existential matters that the denomination currently faces. Therefore, in addition to women's ordination, this book will provide brief discussions on the authority of Scripture and hermeneutics (methods of interpreting the Bible). It will also apply biblical principles to two relevant contemporary issues: homosexuality and abortion.

Third, notwithstanding previous attempts to address the women's ordination conflict, the world church is now so ideologically divided that separation of some divisions and unions from the denomination seem probable. This book offers a biblically based solution to our denomination's present predicament. However, before presenting this solution, I argue that the 2015 San Antonio General Conference Session was a missed opportunity to address women's ordination and related issues in a manner that could bring about lasting change in the world church. In this regard, the San Antonio session was a lukewarm compromise—a compromise with such grave consequences that it is analogous to the Missouri Compromise on slavery in the United States. The Missouri Compromise represented a period of history prior to the Civil War in which slavery remained the status quo in most of the southern states, was prohibited in most of the northern states, but was tolerated in a portion of the mid-western states. This immoral and impractical compromise would inevitably lead to schisms, skirmishes, and the American Civil War. The world church is now in a similar compromise that will likely lead to a major fragmentation.

Fourth, context is very important to the Seventh-day Adventist Church's debate on women's ordination and the other related issues cited above. Thus, before commencing a biblical study on these topics, I tell my story, which provides a context that is germane to our reflection and resolution of these issues. As with all personal accounts, my story will inevitably have a level of subjectivity. Nevertheless, fact and truth emerge out of my story in a manner that justifies the need for this present discourse.

The content of this book is organized into six chapters. **Chapter 1** provides a story of my experience and reflections on women's ordination and related issues from my perspective as a Seventh-day Adventist pastor for thirty years in the New York metropolitan region of the United States of America. This chapter gives a significant context for understanding the rest of the book. The second, third, and fourth chapters of the book discuss the topic of women's ordination from a biblical perspective in a simple user-friendly question-and-answer format. Accordingly, **Chapter 2** focuses on spiritual leadership in the New Testament; it explains the reason for the absence of women in the leadership roles of apostles, elders, and deacons. **Chapter 3** addresses important questions regarding equality, voluntary submission, and gender distinction in the Bible. **Chapter 4** responds to popular claims about women's ordination. **Chapter 5** presents a brief discourse on how the authority of Scripture and hermeneutics are crucial in addressing major contemporary issues such as women's ordination, homosexuality, and abortion. The final chapter, entitled, "A Way Forward," recommends a biblically based solution to the dilemma that the Seventh-day Adventist Church finds itself with respect to the women's ordination controversy and the likelihood of organizational and regional fragmentation.

It is hoped that the reader will find in this book clear biblically based answers to important questions concerning women's ordination and related issues. This hope has a greater chance of being realized if the reader completes the entire book before coming to a final conclusion about the issues it addresses.

Chapter 1

My Story

Before and after Utrecht

As a Seventh-day Adventist pastor for thirty years in the New York metropolitan region, I have been on both sides of the women's ordination issue. In the early 1990s, prior to the 1995 General Conference Session in Utrecht, The Netherlands, I was a supporter of women's ordination. My position at that time was not solidly formed from a study of Scripture. Rather, I gravitated towards some plausible perspectives that I had heard from a few of the esteemed leaders in our denomination. For example, I accepted the argument that, although the Bible does not present a pattern for women as primary spiritual overseers in the church, the promise of Joel 2:28—that God will pour out His spirit on all flesh in the last days—is an indication that God will use women as pastors in the time of the end.

Although my support of women's ordination during this period was not well formed, I never doubted that the issue of women's ordination should be resolved on the basis of *Sola Scriptura*—the Bible and the Bible only. Society's understanding of equality and civil rights should not be a criterion in the church's study and deliberations of the question of women's ordination because the Bible is the ultimate authority in the church.

At some point prior to the Utrecht General Conference Session, I began a biblical study on the topic of women's ordination and concluded that both the Old and New Testaments present a clear pattern for men as primary spiritual overseers—a pattern that Jesus did not overturn even though he could have chosen dedicated female disciples to be among His apostles, such as Mary Magdalene, Joanna, and Susanna (Luke 8:2, 3). I further recognized that, even though the prophecy of Joel 2:28 had its first fulfillment at Pentecost after the outpouring of the Spirit on both male and female disciples, none of the apostles appointed any woman as an apostle, elder, or deacon. This consistent pattern in Scripture led me to search for biblical principles to explain this interesting motif as well as to understand difficult passages that are laden with cultural elements.

Adventists' interpretation of the seventh-day Sabbath became a model of how to properly apply hermeneutics in analyzing passages with cultural elements. Although the Sabbath is often surrounded by cultural and historically local elements, such as references to servants, cattle, and Jewish synagogues (Exod. 20:11; Luke 4:16), Adventists argue that the Sabbath is nevertheless universal and timeless—not limited to the Jews or to ancient times—because it was established at Creation and enjoined in the Ten Commandments. Likewise, I observed that, although there are cultural elements in some of the passages in which Paul restricts the authority of women, these cultural elements do not undermine the principle of male headship because Paul based his argument for the primacy of male spiritual leadership on the order of Creation. For example, in 1 Timothy 2:11, 12, Paul wrote: "Let a woman learn in silence with all submission. And I do not permit a woman to teach or to have authority over a man but to be in silence." Many people claim that this passage is culturally conditioned and, therefore, cannot be applied to the church today. Yet, in verses 13 and 14 of the same chapter, Paul makes it clear that his argument for not permitting women to have spiritual leadership authority over men is based on the Creation order. Notice Paul's words: "For Adam was formed first, then Eve. And Adam was not deceived, but the woman being deceived, fell into transgression" (1 Tim. 2:13, 14). This passage of Scripture cannot be ignored; it should not be relegated to being culturally conditioned. Why? Because the apostle Paul appeals to the Creation for the principle of male headship.

Thus, prior to Utrecht, on the basis of a careful study of Scripture, I concluded that the primacy of male spiritual leadership in the church is rooted in the order that God established at the Creation and is highlighted in both the Old and New Testaments. In similar manner to the popular misconception of the Sabbath as a Jewish norm because of its cultural elements, the passages of Scripture concerning the leadership of women, which appear to be culturally conditioned, are in reality undergirded by the timeless and universal principle of male headship established at the Creation.

Not long after the delegates at Utrecht voted down the proposal from the North American Division (NAD) to allow each division to ordain whom it chose without regard for gender, I had an opportunity to talk with one of the two professors from the Seventh-day Adventist Theological Seminary at Andrews University who made presentations at the session prior to the vote. It appeared that this professor's cogent presentation helped to convince the majority of the delegates to not approve the proposal brought by the NAD to let divisions decide the question of women's ordination within their territories. In any event, this professor shared with me that his conscientious and scholarly presentation aroused the ire of several of his colleagues and other Adventist leaders; they were demonstrably upset with him. In return for his courageous stance, he received the sting of ostracism in an academic community where conscientiousness in theological scholarship is supposed to be valued.

San Antonio and its aftermath

Twenty years later and just a few weeks prior to the 60th General Conference Session in San Antonio, Texas, I began to prepare an open letter to the leadership of the NAD concerning women's ordination. It is important to mention at this juncture that I respect the NAD and I have benefited professionally from their leadership. Therefore, my forthcoming critique of certain aspects of the NAD's leadership should not be construed as an indication of ill will towards the organization. In any event, my open letter was partly in response to a letter that I had received from the NAD, dated January 5, 2015, in which was enclosed a copy of a brochure entitled, "Q&A Theology of Ordination," designed to be shared with local Adventist churches within the NAD's territory. The NAD's letter stated that the brochure "addresses common questions about the topic of ordination." However, after perusing the brochure, I could not in good conscience share it with my congregation because the Seventh-day Adventist denomination had clear protocols in place to address the issue of women's ordination, and the NAD's brochure seemed to preemptively propagandize the issue far beyond the scope of these procedures.

After the delegates at the 60th General Conference Session voted on the evening of July 8, 2015, not to allow each division to decide the question of ordaining women to serve as pastors, I decided that my open letter was no longer necessary because such a vote implied that the world church believes that the Bible does not approve of women serving as primary spiritual overseers in the church. However, when on the morning of July 9, 2015, I read a response by the president of the NAD in the *Adventist Review* to the vote of the General Conference, I concluded that my open letter was more relevant than ever before.

In his response to the General Conference vote, the president of the NAD, Pastor Dan Jackson, claimed to respect the decision of the 60th session and pledged to cooperate with the denomination's actions; however, at the same time, he vitiated and contradicted the obvious sense of his initial statement by further stating, "We will continue with our intention of placing as many women into pastoral ministry as possible."[1] This statement sadly reflects what seems to be the real intention of the leadership of the NAD: to defy the expressed will of the Seventh-day Adventist Church on women's ordination.

The administrators of the NAD have encouraged many dedicated and gifted women to assume the role of pastor with the tantalizing hope that, when leaders and members of the church see that women pastors have already been deployed (and in some cases ordained), the General Conference would be obliged to recognize this as a *fait accompli*. However, this could very well be wishful thinking; it could lead to disappointment for many women pastors. I sympathize with numerous committed women (some of whom I know personally) who have spent years in preparation and service in pastoral ministry but cannot legitimately be ordained. Nevertheless, I also recognize that the leaders who have encouraged these women down this road bear enormous responsibility for their suffering.

For the past five years since the 2015 General Conference Session, the leadership of the NAD continued with its "intention of placing as many women into pastoral ministry as possible." The NAD has also tacitly endorsed all previous actions taken by union conferences in its territory to ordain women as pastors. Furthermore, the NAD's strategy to place as many women as possible into pastoral ministry will likely set the stage for a move toward individualism and congregationalism within its own territory. Local congregations and local leaders might gradually follow the

---

[1]Daniel Jackson, *Adventist Review*, July 9, 2015.

NAD's example in rendering lip service to the decision of the 60th General Conference Session while, at the same time, strategically circumnavigating the expressed will of the Seventh-day Adventist Church. Once the precedence of defying legitimate authority is set in motion then the gate will be wide open for churches, conferences, unions, and divisions to follow their own agendas at the expense of unity and truth.

There are several examples of unions that have followed the NAD's lead in resisting the will of the General Conference in the aftermath of the San Antonio session. The propensity to act independently may be seen in the actions revolving around

The NAD's strategy to place as many women as possible into pastoral ministry will likely set the stage for a move toward individualism and congregationalism within its own territory.

the North Pacific Union Conference's (NPUC) scheduling of a constituency meeting on women's ordination in the aftermath of the San Antonio session. A few union conference leaders and top officials in the NAD had misconstrued a clause in the General Conference Working Policy in a way that supposedly gives license for unions to have jurisdiction over the issue of women's ordination. When the General Conference administration clarified the aforementioned clause, NPUC realized that its attempts to act on women's ordination would represent a departure from both the San Antonio vote and the General Conference Working Policy. Therefore, on August 19, 2015, NPUC voted to rescind its previous decision to hold a constituency meeting on women's ordination. However, NPUC voted on the same day to increase opportunities for women in pastoral ministry and leadership in its territory.[2] NPUC clearly followed the NAD's lead in paying lip service to the 60th General Conference Session's decision on women's ordination.

One month after NPUC's actions, the executive committee of the Norwegian Union voted on September 20, 2015, to discontinue the practice of ordination altogether. Obviously, this was done in order to circumnavigate the 60th General Conference decision on women's ordination. Union conferences in Sweden, Denmark, and the Netherlands have all

---

[2]"U.S. Union Conference Rescinds Special Meeting on Women's Ordination," *Adventist Review*, online edition, August 20, 2015.

voted similar policies around the same time as Norway. Although their actions undermine the will of the Seventh-day Adventist denomination, these unions believe that they have circumvented the issue of women's ordination. However, unions do not have the authority to unilaterally take such actions with respect to ordination. These actions clearly undermine the expressed will of the denomination in the San Antonio General Conference Session.

Based on my observation and interactions with several of our leaders in NAD territory, the 60th General Conference vote seems to be an obstacle that some of our administrators are prepared to surmount, ignore, or defy in order to achieve the goal of women's ordination. The momentum for defying the vote of the 60th General Conference Session has picked up pace in recent years, sometimes in reverberating ways, such as the appointment in February 2020 of a female as the Director of the Doctor of Ministry program at the Seventh-day Adventist Theological Seminary at Andrews University.

The core of the San Antonio compromise

As I was preparing my open letter in the days following the 60th General Conference Session, I became more and more convinced that this document should not only be addressed to the North American Division but also to the leadership of the General Conference. My reason for this was that top administrators of our denomination had an opportunity to lead our world church to deal with the whole question of whether or not the Bible permits the ordination of women as primary spiritual overseers in the offices of pastor, elder, and deacon. However, after facilitating more than two years of a process that entailed a biblical study and deliberation on the theology of ordination, our administrators chose not to put forth the women's ordination question as a biblical issue in the San Antonio General Conference Session. They merely construed the question in a way that emphasized political and cultural expedience.

The task of leading our world church is certainly not easy. Our leaders often face harsh criticisms. Sometimes the politicization of our democratic process tends to prevent a biblical matter from being settled on the basis of Scriptural principles. The leaders of the General Conference should be commended for facilitating a fair and biblically grounded process for the study and deliberation of women's ordination in the years leading up to the 60th session. However, considering the fact that both delegates and non-delegates gathered in San Antonio to deal with a theological/biblical question, for which the denomination had spent more than two years preparing to address, it has baffled me why our administrators permitted a proposal to be put forth at the 60th session that had only a tangential relation to a theological/biblical question. This seems to represent an insidious failure in leadership, especially when one considers that the question of whether or not divisions should be permitted to ordain women in their territories had already been settled at the General Conference Session in Utrecht in 1995.

Let us examine the proposition that was presented to the delegates at the 60th General Conference Session. Here it is:

> Is it acceptable for division executive committees, as they may deem it appropriate in their territories, to make provision for the ordination of women to the gospel ministry? Yes or No.

The above proposition was preceded by another clause which suggested that the delegates should base their decision on a prayerful study of the Bible and the writings of Ellen G. White. However, the wording of the above proposition itself focuses on the appropriateness of the divisions of the world church to provide for women's ordination, rather than on whether or not on the basis of Scripture women can be ordained as pastors, elders, and deacons. Again, the proposition itself ironically deals with a political question, while the process that was used to facilitate the study of women's ordination attempted to address the issue from a biblical standpoint. There is only a tangential connection between the proposition and the process used to address the issue.

Let us assume, based on the information gathered by the Theology of Ordination Study Committee, that both proponents and the opponents of women's ordination on TOSC agreed that there is no substantive biblical distinction between the office of pastor and elder. If this be the case, it is reasonable to contend that the leadership of the 60th session should have brought this issue to the floor. In our denomination, a pastor is essentially a supervising elder. Both the pastor and the local elder are ordained to fulfill virtually the same job description. The main difference between the two is in authority and scope—namely, pastors are not elected by the local church, as is the case of elders, and pastors have greater authority and a wider field of governance than local elders. Given the theological equivalence of pastors and elders, why did our world church administrators neglect to deal with the question of whether or not, on the basis of

Scripture, women may be ordained as elders? This question is inextricably connected to the main question concerning ordaining women.

It bears mentioning that the decision to ordain women as elders was not approved by a vote at a quinquennium General Conference session. Rather, it was sanctioned by a vote at the Spring Council in 1975 and then reaffirmed at the Annual Council in 1984. This watershed decision was made "under the radar" of the watchful eyes of the larger body of believers who usually attend the quinquennium sessions of the General Conference. Such an important and momentous change in ministerial and ecclesiastical practice should have been reserved for a General Conference session, not an Annual Council meeting.

At San Antonio, our administrators, by depriving us of a discussion of the offices of elders and deacons in the women's ordination proposal, missed an opportunity to allow God to stretch the mind, faith, and courage of His people. Our leaders seem to have settled for a smoother path, yet one that brings us back to the same place as we were in 1995 at Utrecht. We as a church made no meaningful progress, for, although many members sincerely approached the women's ordination question with earnest prayer and study, the denomination barely stretched beyond where it was in 1995 because of its neglect to comprehensively deal with the women's ordination question, especially as it relates to the overseer roles of elders and deacons.

One of the things that could have come from a comprehensive discussion of ordination as it relates to pastors, elders, and deacons is a new appreciation for, and an emphasis on, the administrative role of a deacon. As I will argue later, in the New Testament, the deacon is an administrator in charge of caring for people's physical, material, and spiritual needs. Deacons shared in the administrative work of the apostles and elders in the early New Testament church. However, in many of our churches today, deacons are viewed merely as caretakers of the physical plant and as a team of workers to assist in communion, baptism, and visitation. They are rarely placed in administrative roles such as leaders of community outreach, finance, and music in the church.

Another important part of such a discussion might have been the way in which women church leaders can collaborate with men who are serving in the spiritual overseer roles of pastors, elders, and deacons. Such a discussion would have naturally led to the following question: How did prophetesses work with the primary spiritual leaders of the church in biblical times?

The General Conference administration's failure to lead the church in addressing women's ordination in a comprehensive way leaves the door ajar for this issue to come back. When the early New Testament church called a general council in Jerusalem to deal with the question of whether or not Gentile converts were required to be circumcised, the leaders dealt with the issue on the basis of the harmony between Scripture and the leading of the Holy Spirit. The matter was handled in a comprehensive way. The question was settled, and the church moved on. By contrast, at the 60th General Conference Session, our leaders chose a compromised proposition that only tangentially addressed the theological and biblical question. Can anyone doubt that this matter will return to the world church again? Should we not have dealt with the issue as thoroughly as possible, no matter how long it took, patiently waiting upon God for guidance? This would have been better than what now exists: namely, a compromised status quo that only forestalls the women's ordination issue and robbed the denomination of a golden opportunity to depend wholly upon God for direction.

Let us remember that essentially the same kind of proposal that was voted on at the 60th session had been presented to the delegates in 1995 at Utrecht. As mentioned, at Utrecht, the debate on women's ordination came as a result of a request by the North American Division that each division be given the latitude to ordain without regard to gender. This proposal was voted down. Twenty years later, virtually the same proposal was presented to the delegates in San Antonio and once again it was voted down. What is going to keep this issue from coming back?

Interestingly, the statement of the president of the General Conference concerning the meaning of the San Antonio vote is tantamount to a virtual concession to the fact that we, as a world church, have not made any progress on the women's ordination issue. The General Conference president represented the 60th session's decision as a mere return to our dubious policy in which we do not ordain women as pastors, but we do ordain them as local elders. Hence, after at least four years of preparation and deliberation on the women's ordination issue, we came back to the same unenlightened, impractical, and compromised position that we settled for at Utrecht in 1995.

It is clear to me, from my personal observation of the debate and the vote on women's ordination on July 8, 2015, that the will of the majority of the delegates was to not approve women's ordination. However, due to what appears to be a mismanagement by our top administrators, the only proposition that was permitted to be voted on was whether or not we should allow divisions to have the authority to decide the question of women's ordination in their respective territories. The will of the majority was muffled. Consequently, we are currently in such a compromised position that some of us will see in the 60th General Conference decision the expressed will of the denomination against women's ordination while others will see in it a mere return to our dubious policy of permitting women to serve as pastors but not allowing them to be ordained. This is the epitome of confusion. It is leading to fragmentation and unilateral actions in various corners of our world church.

As an example of some of the schisms emanating from the 2015 General Conference Session, an article dated August 17, 2015, in *Spectrum* magazine reported an incident under the caption, "Florida Conference Calls Doug Batchelor a 'Polarizing Influence,' Discourages Speaking Appointment." The article describes how Pastor Mike Cauley, the then president of the Florida Conference, discouraged the Spring Meadow Church in Sanford, Florida, from following through with inviting Pastor Doug Batchelor, Speaker/Director of Amazing Facts Ministries, to come for a scheduled week-long series of meetings in October 2–10, 2015. The reason given for such a call to disinvite a well-respected pastor and evangelist, was that, according to Cauley and the Florida Conference Administration, "Pastor Batchelor" is "a polarizing influence in the Seventh-day Adventist Church" because he has taught against ordaining women as pastors and local elders for several years.[3] Cauley and the Florida Conference Administration claimed that Bachelor's position "is not in harmony with the policy of the General Conference of Seventh-day Adventists," which encourages "women to use the gifts God has given them for ministry, both as local elders and in pastoral leadership and ministry."[4]

While there may be valid reasons on both sides for disagreement in the above controversy, the fact that a bona fide Adventist pastor can be disinvited from doing a series of evangelistic meetings because of his convictions about women's ordination is a travesty. But what further compounds this conflict is that a conference president in the North American Division justified this egregious action by appealing to the policies of the General Conference. This incident has the makings of ideological bias

---

[3]Mike Cauley quoted in, "Florida Conference Calls Doug Batchelor a 'Polarizing Influence,' Discourages Speaking Appointment," *Spectrum Magazine*, Aug. 17, 2015.
[4]Cauley, *Spectrum Magazine*, Aug. 17, 2015.

and strategic use of the inconsistent practices and policies of the world church to further one's narrow agenda. After a series of actions in the NAD prior to the 2015 General Conference Session—such as the unilateral decisions of the Columbia Union Conference and the Pacific Union Conference to ordain women pastors even while the world church was in the process of studying the issue, the improper election of the president of the Southeastern California Conference, and the stated intention of the president of the North American Division to encourage as many women as possible to become pastors—no one should be surprised by incidents such as what occurred between the Florida Conference administration and Pastor Batchelor. We might as well expect that such incidents will increase unless the leaders of our denomination act decisively.

The numerous public incidents of independent and sometimes rebellious actions by leaders of divisions, unions, local conferences, and local churches that have taken place in the wake of the San Antonio General Conference Session reinforce a conclusion that I arrived at in the closing days of the 60th General Conference Session: namely, that in San Antonio our leaders made a compromise that is as consequential for the Seventh-day Adventist Church as the Missouri Compromise was for the Civil War in the United States. As has been mentioned, the Missouri Compromise was an immoral and impractical solution for the issue of slavery. In the Missouri Compromise, slavery would remain the status quo in most of the southern states, it would be excluded in most of the northern states, and it would be tolerated in some mid-western states. Such an unscrupulous and shortsighted remedy to the issue of slavery spawned dissimulations, clandestine operations, and outright civil war. Likewise, the San Antonio Compromise on women's ordination has already generated schisms and skirmishes that might also explode into permanent fragmentation of the denomination.

The progressive deconstructionist movement

While some proponents of women's ordination are sincerely focused on addressing that particular issue alone, there are other leaders in various echelons of the church for whom women's ordination is only one component of a broader project. Their project involves deconstructing historic/ traditional Adventism and reconstructing it into a new image that is more consistent with a social justice, ecumenical, charismatic, and progressive direction. This project espouses some things that seem very positive, such as "social justice." Given the shameful discriminatory practices of the Seventh-day Adventist Church toward Blacks in the past—especially during the Civil Rights Era of the 1950s and 1960s in the United States—racial equality and justice is something that our world church definitely needs to be passionate about. But the problem with the social justice platform of the progressive wing of Adventism is that it is more beholden to the philosophies and ideologies of contemporary society than it is to the authority of Scripture.

> *The problem with the social justice platform of the progressive wing of Adventism is that it is more beholden to the philosophies and ideologies of contemporary society than it is to the authority of Scripture.*

In order to be in alignment with contemporary sentiments and ideologies, many of our leaders are ready to undermine principles of hermeneutics that Adventist scholars and lay people have relied on for approximately 170 years. These leaders have chosen to espouse a cultural and relativistic interpretation of several biblical passages that deal with the primacy of male spiritual leadership in the home and the church. They have reduced the authority of Scripture to be able to accommodate a gender equality platform that ignores fundamental biblical principles concerning leadership that were established at Creation.

As an example, during the intensives for my Doctor of Ministry program at Andrews University (2014–2017), I witnessed on different occasions more than one professor attempting to shift the class away from Adventism's emphasis on discovering the truth through a diligent study of Scripture, proper hermeneutics, and reliance on the Holy Spirit. These professors subtly advocated subjective interpretations, cultural relativism, and an excessive dependence on the "Spirit" rather than on the Bible.

The progressive deconstructionist movement in Adventism seems to have its epicenter in the North American Division, and it has been this way for nearly fifty years. However, its ideology now reverberates loudly in most of the unions and divisions in Western Europe. In order for the progressive deconstructionists to gain support for women's ordination, they have to weaken the authority of Scripture with claims that certain passages are culturally conditioned and that we need to lean more on the Spirit than on a literal interpretation of Scripture. However, these very claims have also opened the door for an accommodationist approach toward homosexuality and the LGBT community within the Seventh-day Adventist denomination.

The accommodationist approach toward homosexuality emphasizes that the church needs to be more accepting, understanding, and gracious toward those with homosexual, bisexual, and transgender tendencies. They call on the church to provide support groups for the LGBT community and to not ostracize them from its fellowship. While I agree that the church should be more understanding and gracious toward people who are struggling with homosexual, bisexual, and transgender proclivities, the church is not called to be an accepting community of the homosexual lifestyle. Moreover, there is a world of difference between a person who is struggling with homosexual tendencies but is seeking divine deliverance and a gay person who is looking for acceptance from the church rather than conversion.

Two subtexts emanate from the accommodationist approach toward homosexuality. The first subtext is that sensitivity towards gay and transgendered people means that we should not preach a sermon, make a remark, or write an essay against the sin of homosexuality because this could be very offensive to the LGBT community. According to this approach, pastors should not preach Paul's powerfully convicting message in the first chapter of Romans, which explicitly states that the judgment of God will fall on unrepentant human beings who sexually cohabitate with another person of the same gender. Homosexuality is depicted as unnatural and vile in Romans 1. There are people who are tempted to engage in the gay lifestyle out of mere curiosity because it is in vogue; Paul's message in Romans 1 might very well prevent them from going down such a path. However, the accommodationist approach does not offer "prevention" as an option. It merely offers a dubious acceptance.

The second subtext is that conversion or transformation is not a realistic option for the LGBT community and that we should, therefore, simply accept this community and be willing to let them serve as officers in the church as long as they do not *publicly* engage in homosexuality. One example of the practical impact of this subtext may be seen in the activities of Intercollegiate Adventist Gay-Straight Coalition (IAGC), an organization that has been created since 2012 to support members of the LGBTQ community within Seventh-day Adventist institutions of higher learning. Although IAGC is not an official entity of the Seventh-day Adventist Church, it has a presence on several Adventist campuses, including Andrews University, La Sierra University, Pacific Union College, Southern Adventist University, Union College, Walla Walla University, and Washington Adventist University. Although Andrews University has had an official LGBT support group since October 2017, this support group is also affiliated with IACC.[5] One of my colleagues attended a meeting of the LGBT support group on the campus of Andrews University in early 2020. This meeting was advertised specifically as a forum to converse with parents of LGBTQ students. However, my colleague was surprised to discover that the leaders of this support group were intentionally advocating that LGBTQ orientations were a natural biological condition that LGBTQ members should accept rather than seek to be converted from. My colleague also reported that the leaders in this meeting told the audience not to offer prayer for transformation of the LGBTQ community, but, rather, that they should accept the members of that community. It is also noteworthy that, in its promotional media, IAGC does not mention, as one of its objectives, anything about conversion or transformation from a same-sex orientation.[6]

The rhetorical catalyst for the accommodationist view of homosexuality seems to have come from a conference held in January 2006 in Ontario, California, which was co-sponsored by the Seventh-day Adventist Kinship International Advisory Council and the Association of Adventist Forums. This conference resulted in a book that posited a revisionist view of homosexuality—one that is in stark contrast to the mainstream perspective of Seventh-day Adventists on the topic. The book, published in 2008, is entitled *Christianity and Homosexuality: Some Seventh-day Adventist Perspectives*.[7] Partly in response to the conference in California and the subsequent book, a new conference was held by a variety of Christian scholars and professionals at Andrews University in 2009. This conference sought to evaluate the merits of the new revisionist perspective of homosexuality and to discuss the implications of the standard Adventist position on the topic with respect to social developments and public policy. The

---

[5]Alisa Williams, "Andrews University Approves Creation of Official LGBT Student Support Group," *Spectrum Magazine*, Nov. 9, 2017, retrieved from https://1ref.us/1cm, accessed 8/20/20.

[6]See the following: Eliel Cruz, "Seventh-day Adventist Students Sharing Stories," retrieved from https://1ref.us/1cn, accessed 8/20/20; Richard Logan, "Southern Adventist University Student Now Leads LGBT Collegiate Coalition," *Spectrum Magazine*, Oct. 23, 2014, retrieved from https://1ref.us/1co, accessed 8/20/20; Andy Roman, "The LGBT+ is Making More Inroads into the Seventh-day Adventist Educational Institutions," *Advent Messenger*, Dec. 7, 2018, retrieved from https://1ref.us/1cp, accessed 8/20/20.

[7]David Ferguson, Fritz Guy, David Larson, eds., *Christianity and Homosexuality: Some Seventh-day Adventist Perspectives* (Adventist Forum, 2008).

participants of this conference provided strong biblical support for the historic Adventist position on homosexuality. They also discussed ways for the church to minister more effectively to the LGBT community. The papers and presentations of the 2009 conference at Andrews University formed the content for a solid and perspicacious book that was published in 2012, entitled *Homosexuality, Marriage, and the Church*.[8]

In October 2015, the Seventh-day Adventist Theological Seminary at Andrews University published a position paper entitled, "An Understanding of the Biblical View on Homosexual Practice and Pastoral Care: Seventh-day Adventist Theological Seminary Position Paper." More than three-fourths of the paper supports the historic Adventist position on homosexuality. However, toward the end of the paper, there is a major departure from the standard Adventist perspective. The paper asserts that homosexual persons should be allowed to have membership in the Seventh-day Adventist Church if that is what they desired even if they struggle with same-sex temptations. In addition, it asserts that gay and lesbian members should be permitted to serve as officers of the church if they will choose to remain abstinent from engaging in same-sex cohabitation.[9]

The apostle Paul clearly declared that God's power transformed people who were formerly homosexuals into committed heterosexual members of the church in Corinth. Paul stated, in 1 Corinthians 6:9, 10: "Neither fornicators, nor idolaters, nor adulterers, nor homosexuals, nor sodomites, nor thieves, nor covetous, nor drunkards, nor revilers, nor extortioners will inherit the kingdom of God." Then he emphasized in verse 11 that some of the current believers of the church in Corinth were once engaged in these immoral lifestyles but that they had since been cleansed, converted, and sanctified. Notice Paul's words: "And such were some of you. But you were washed, but you were sanctified, but you were justified in the name of the Lord Jesus and by the Spirit of God." Divine transformation is not merely possible for homosexuals, adulterers, and idolaters—it is the only option for those who intend to inherit the kingdom of God.

The problem with the position paper from the Seventh-day Adventist Theological Seminary at Andrews University is that it blurs the line

---

[8]Roy E. Gane, Nicholas P. Miller, H. Peter Swanson, eds., *Homosexuality, Marriage, and the Church: Biblical, Counseling and Religious Liberty Issues* (Berrien Springs, MI: Andrews University Press, 2012).

[9]"An Understanding of the Biblical View on Homosexual Practice and Pastoral Care: Seventh-day Adventist Theological Seminary Position Paper" (Berrien Springs, MI: Seventh-day Adventist Theological Seminary, October 9, 2015), retrieved from https://1ref.us/1cq, accessed 8/20/20.

between the person who was once a homosexual but has been transformed by the power of God and the person who believes that he or she can be a Seventh-day Adventist Christian and yet have a same-sex orientation. A person who was formerly a homosexual and has been transformed is no longer a homosexual. The common notion in society that can be expressed as, "Once an alcoholic, always an alcoholic," is not a biblical principle. Moreover, if a person has been converted and he or she still genuinely struggles with feelings of same-sex attraction, this is no indication that the person is a homosexual; it is an indication that converted people still have to struggle with the carnal nature. Numerous passages of Scripture speak about the daily battle of believers to crucify the flesh and walk in the Spirit with the assurance that we can be successful through the power of Christ and the Spirit (see Matt. 5:27–30; Rom. 6:1–23; 8:5–13; 1 Cor. 9:24–27; 2 Cor. 10:3–5; Gal. 2:20; 5:1–21; 6:7, 8; James 1:14, 15; Phil. 2:12, 13; 4:11–13; 1 Peter 4:1, 2). Thus, the conclusion of the Seventh-day Adventist Theological Seminary position paper is essentially a concession to the power of the flesh rather than of the Spirit.

What the NAD and its constituent unions, conferences, and institutions believe about homosexuality will impact how they allocate funds and deploy resources. For example, if the leadership of a particular conference or union believes that the LBGT community cannot be converted and that the church would be better-off to not preach about the sin of homosexuality but to accept the LGBT community as a biological *fait accompli,* then it will not utilize or allocate funds to any kind of conversion program such as Coming Out Ministries or a conversion based support group; rather, it will focus its resources on programs that teach acceptance of the LGBT community. Moreover, employees who are not in support of a conference, union, or constituent institution's accommodationist approach toward homosexuality will likely experience undue pressure to conform or be ostracized.

The gradual erosion of biblical authority that has been unleashed by the progressive deconstructionist movement in Adventism is virtually aiding and abetting a state of affairs in which leaders and members do what they believe is right in their own eyes with little regard for the principles of Scripture and guidance from the writings of Ellen G. White. For example, the practice of abortion on demand has been facilitated as a matter of routine in several Adventist hospitals in the United States within the past four decades. However, popular indignation from vocal Adventists, especially in 2018 and 2019, have aroused the leaders of the denomination to take steps to curtail this practice.[10]

Another example of the liberal pluralism unleashed by the progressive deconstructionists is that a growing segment of Adventists are imitating unbiblical practices derived from the Charismatic Movement, Eastern religions, and popular music in their worship services. Whooping accompanied by organ rifts, mindless meditation, prolonged and heavily rhythmic music with sustained loud sounding instruments, and a variety of frenzied outbursts are some of the elements that are now present in numerous Adventist worship services.

Some of the new churches that have recently been established in the NAD's territory have been planted by leaders who are intentionally deconstructing Adventism and reconstructing new local churches according to progressive ideology. In some of these churches, the criteria for membership fall far below the standards that the Seventh-day Adventist denomination has clearly explained in the church manual and in the book containing its fundamental beliefs, *Seventh-day Adventists Believe.*

Unless bold decisive actions are soon taken the denomination will follow the path of several mainline Protestant denominations that have bartered faithfulness to Scripture for favor with the world.

I did not imagine in 1983, when as a teenager I surrendered my life to Jesus Christ and became a Seventh-day Adventist, that the "remnant" church would be so tempted to veer from its faithful adherence to the full authority of Scripture and the historical-grammatical method of Bible interpretation. I could not then foresee that numerous pastors and leaders would be so accommodative towards popular practices and ideologies that cannot be supported by Scripture. The Seventh-day Adventist Church is now at a crossroads as it prepares to convene the 61st General Conference Session. The actions voted at the San Antonio General

[10]See George B. Gainer, "Abortion: history of Adventist guidelines," *Ministry*, Aug. 1991, retrieved from https://1ref.us/1cr, accessed 8/20/20; Michael Peabody, "Amidst Growing Criticism Adventist Church Is Revisiting Abortion Position," *Spectrum*, Sept 23, 2019, retrieved from https://1ref.us/1cs, accessed 8/20/20; Dylan Wagoner, "The Day I Found Out About Abortions in SDA Hospitals (Part 1)," fulcrum7.com, blogpost, Aug. 23, 2019, retrieved from https://1ref.us/1ct, accessed 8/20/20; "Statement on the Biblical View of Unborn Life and its Implications of Abortion," General Conference, Oct. 2019, retrieved from https://1ref.us/1cu, accessed 8/20/20.

Conference Session were grossly inadequate to stem the tidal wave that is now beating ferociously on the banks of this denomination. Unless bold decisive actions are soon taken the denomination will follow the path of several mainline Protestant denominations that have bartered faithfulness to Scripture for favor with the world.

Three decades ago, C. Raymond Holmes, former Director of the Doctor of Ministry Program and Professor of Worship and Preaching in the Seventh-day Adventist Theological Seminary at Andrews University, presciently cautioned the Seventh-day Adventist Church against devaluing the authority of Scripture in order to win support for women's ordination. In his book, *The Tip of an Iceberg*, Holmes shared how, as a former pastor in the Lutheran Church in America, his denomination's espousal of the skeptical historical-critical method of Bible interpretation led it to embrace women's ordination in the 1970s; conversely, the Lutheran Church-Missouri Synod's strong rejection of the historical-critical method influenced its rejection of women's ordination.[11]

What is even more interesting is that all the liberal branches of the Lutheran denomination in America that embraced the historical-critical method and women's ordination in the 1960s and 70s currently endorse homosexual clergy. For example, the Evangelical Lutheran Church in America (now the largest body of Lutherans in the USA, which was formed in 1988 as the result of the merging of the three most liberal Lutheran branches in North America), began accepting gay clergy in 2009 and elected its first openly gay bishop in 2013. However, the Lutheran Church-Missouri Synod, which is the second largest Lutheran body in the United States, still rejects the historical-critical method, women's ordination, and homosexuality.

The progression from the adoption of a limited view of biblical authority to the ordination of women and then to approving same-sex marriage has also occurred within the Episcopal Church, the Presbyterian Church USA, the United Church of Christ, and the Unitarian Universalist Association of Churches. If we do not take decisive steps to "contend for the faith" by rejecting specious notions that undermine the authority of Scripture, such as the culturally conditioned argument, it is very probable that the Seventh-day Adventist Church will follow in a similar direction as these churches.

---

[11]C. Raymond Holmes, *The Tip of an Iceberg: Biblical Authority, Biblical Interpretation, and the Ordination of Women in Ministry* (Wakefield, Michigan: Pointer Publications, 1994).

One glaring example of the downward slope of the progressive deconstructionist/accommodationist approach in Adventism is that Adventist Health System/West, a corporation of Seventh-day Adventist healthcare institutions on the west coast of the United States, has authorized and conducted gender transition services at its facilities. Physicians governed by Adventist Health System/West can provide hormone therapy to facilitate changes in gender, perform gender affirming surgery, and make referrals for gender reconstruction surgery. In other words, this large Seventh-day Adventist affiliated healthcare corporation is helping males to acquire hormones and physical alterations in order to function as females, and helping females to transition into what appear to be males. This information was exhibited on November 22, 2019 in a set of documents prepared by the California Attorney General office and Adventist Health System/West, as Adventist Health System/West prepared to acquire Delano Regional Medical Center.[12]

After prayerful reflection on the most prudent and respectful way to address the concerns that I have highlighted above, I decided to change my intended open letter into a brief book that is designed to do the following four things: (1) provide a biblical study on the topic of women's ordination, (2) show how the question of women's ordination is related to other vitally important contemporary issues in the church, (3) recommend a possible solution to the dilemma that Adventism finds itself in, (4) tell my story. Having told my story in this chapter, the rest of the book will cover the first three objectives.

---

[12]Xavier Becerra, Attorney General, State of California Department of Justice, letter to Mark Schieble, Nov 22, 2019, RE: "Proposed change in control and governance of Central California Foundation for Health," https://1ref.us/1ja (accessed January 25, 2021). See also Andy Roman, "Adventist Health Allows its Physicians to Perform 'Gender Transition' Services at it Facilities." *Advent Messenger*, December 26, 2020, https://1ref.us/1jb (accessed January 25, 2021).

Chapter 2

Spiritual Leadership in the New Testament

Is the example of Jesus and the apostles in setting apart only men as apostles, elders, and deacons based on biblical principles or the culture of the period?

The narratives of the four gospels show that Jesus Christ chose and mentored twelve men as apostles for the purpose of leading the New Testament church. They also show that these twelve apostles were chosen out of a larger body of disciples that included both males and females. Accordingly, Luke 6:13 states thus, "And when it was day, He called His disciples to Himself; and from them He chose twelve whom He also named apostles."

We know that both Jesus and John the Baptist had disciples, but, of the two, it is said only of Jesus that he chose twelve of his disciples out of a larger body to be His apostles. John the Baptist's disciples were to collaborate with him in preparing the way for the Messiah, and it was the Messiah's mission not only to save humanity but also to forge the principle of leadership that would govern His church until He returns. Jesus was just as intentional about mentoring the twelve apostles to govern the church as He was about saving humanity. The setting apart of twelve men as apostles was not an incidental event that was tied to custom or culture; it was essential to the governance of the Christian church.

The great Gospel Commission of Matthew 28:19, 20 entails making disciples for Jesus Christ. Hence, the church is composed of disciples of Christ, and the church is commissioned to make disciples for Jesus. The New Testament reveals that all the disciples who entered the church after Jesus' ascension were governed by the universal leadership of Christ's apostles and the local leadership of elders/bishops, and deacons—all of whom were males. Later on, we will discuss the significance of the selection of deacons in Acts 6, the leadership of the Jerusalem Council of Acts 15, and Paul's instruction concerning the qualifications for local elders and deacons. However, what is important at this juncture is to underscore the fact that Jesus' selection and mentoring of twelve men to be entrusted with the responsibility of overseeing the church, including shaping its polity, was not accidental or merely a matter of culture but a part of God's design.

The argument for Mary's inclusion in the spiritual leadership of the church is virtually on the same level as the argument for Sunday to be observed as a day of worship in honor of the resurrection: they both seem plausible on the surface, but they are really specious and without biblical foundation.

Jesus' selection of only male apostles

The Bible records several notable female disciples who cared for Jesus out of their substance during His labors, prepared spices to anoint His body after His death, and were the first to behold the resurrected Christ and to proclaim this good news to some of the apostles. They included Mary Magdalene, Joanna, and Susanna (see Luke 8:2, 3; Mark 15:40, 41; Matt. 28:1, 9, 10; Luke 24:9–11). However, Jesus did not give leadership authority to any of these illustrious women. Certainly, none of these faithful godly women were set apart by Christ or the apostles to be apostles, elders, or deacons in the New Testament church. Although it is commonly argued that, in specifically instructing Mary Magdalene to tell the other disciples that He is risen and that they should meet Him in Galilee, Christ was symbolically commissioning the first woman to the leadership position of an ordained minister, there is no evidence in all of the New Testament that suggests that Mary Magdalene was ever set apart by Jesus or any of the apostles to be an apostle, elder, or deacon. The argument for Mary's inclusion in the spiritual leadership of the church is virtually on the same level as the argument for Sunday to be observed as a day of worship in honor of the resurrection: they both seem plausible on the surface, but they are really specious and without biblical foundation.

Notice again that, while Jesus had several hundred active disciples during His three and a half years of public ministry on earth, only twelve of them were always with Him. The Gospel of Mark states: "Then He appointed twelve, that they might be with Him and that He might send them out to preach" (Mark 3:14). There were other disciples who assisted Jesus in his ministry, but they were not consistently with Jesus like the twelve. The twelve left their previous occupations to be trained for a special leadership role in the Messiah's church. So special was the role the twelve were to occupy that the apostles, after Jesus' ascension, made sure that they asked God to select another apostle to fill the post that Judas once occupied.

> *If Mary Magdalene were scripturally qualified to be included as one of the apostles, the apostles would certainly have accepted her into that role after having accepted Mathias, Paul, and Barnabas as apostles.*

Moreover, it appears that a main qualification to be among the twelve founding apostles was that the candidate had to be personally mentored by Jesus Christ. Accordingly, the candidates that the apostles put forward to be chosen to replace Judas had to meet this criterion (Acts 1:21–26). Later on, when Paul made known to the apostles that he had personally encountered the resurrected Christ and was subsequently taught by Him, they accepted him also as one of the apostles with the same authority as the twelve. Furthermore, Barnabas is specifically referred to as an apostle in Acts 14:14. Thus, in the New Testament, the primary qualification for apostleship seems to be a male disciple who was either mentored by Jesus Christ Himself or by one of the apostles who had been mentored by

Jesus (Acts 1:21, 22). It is also not unreasonable to infer that the seventy disciples whom Jesus specifically appointed to conduct the same missionary work as the twelve were also apostles and that Jesus himself had mentored them (Luke 10:1–11; 9:1–6).

If Mary Magdalene were scripturally qualified to be included as one of the apostles, the apostles would certainly have accepted her into that role after having accepted Mathias, Paul, and Barnabas as apostles. After all, Mary was a close friend of Jesus; she traveled with Him; she was the first to see the resurrected Christ; there is no doubt that, if she met the biblical criteria, she would have been set apart for that role of leadership.

Some people have argued that Jesus acquiesced to the culture of His times to the extent that He did not include women as spiritual overseers in the church. However, such an assertion is essentially specious when we consider that the New Testament reveals Jesus as a person who boldly challenged the status quo of both culture and of the religious establishment. For example, He publicly ministered to Gentiles in addition to Jews, which was not a common practice among the exclusive Jewish establishment of Jesus' day. Also, He preached and taught without ever attending the rabbinical schools of His time. Moreover, Jesus was very intentional about spiritual leadership in the church as can be seen in His appointing and mentoring of the twelve apostles. Spiritual leadership is not an area in which Jesus would merely accommodate culture. Ephesians 5:23 clearly states that "Christ is head of the church." He is not the tail but the head. We can rest assured that the "head" knew what He was doing when He set apart twelve male apostles as the nucleus of spiritual overseers in the church.

The apostles' selection of only male deacons

In the New Testament, the twelve apostles had a special founding role in Christ's church—a role that gave them the authority to shape the polity of the church in accordance with what they had learned from Jesus and in harmony with the leading of the Holy Spirit. Did the apostles do anything substantively different than what they had learned from Jesus with respect to selecting overseers and other leaders in the church? The answer to this question is an unequivocal "no." They chose males as the spiritual overseers of the church: namely, as apostles, elders/bishops, and deacons.

The book of Acts shows that the twelve apostles and Paul governed the work of the early New Testament church with the help of deacons and local elders. In Acts, chapter 6, a complaint arose against the Hebrew

Christians (Palestinian Jewish converts) from the Hellenists Christians (converts of Greek-speaking Jews from the diaspora) that the Hellenist widows were being neglected in the distribution of funds and goods. The twelve apostles, realizing that their direct supervision of the distribution would take away time and energy from more important responsibilities of spiritual leadership, delegated leadership responsibility to seven men as deacons.

Let us notice how the apostles directed the multitude of disciples in Jerusalem to choose seven men according to the criteria outlined by the apostles. In this biblical description, we have harmony between the primary governance of the apostles and the representative electoral selection of the constituency of disciples:

> Then the twelve summoned the multitude of the disciples and said, "It is not desirable that we should leave the word of God and serve tables. Therefore, brethren, seek out from among you seven men of good reputation, full of the Holy Spirit and wisdom, whom we may appoint over this business; but we will give ourselves continually to prayer and to the ministry of the word." (Acts 6:2–4)

The multitude of disciples were pleased with the apostles' directives (Acts 6:5) and made their selection according to the criteria given by the apostles. The multitude chose seven men "full of faith and the Holy Spirit" and "set them before the apostles," and the apostles prayed and laid hands on the seven men (Acts 6:5, 6). The selection of the deacons is consistent with what the twelve apostles had learned from Jesus and also with how Moses had delegated leadership authority to seventy chosen men when the burden of governing the nation of Israel was too much for him to bear. Acts, chapters 6–8, show that the job description of deacons was similar to the work of the seventy male elders that assisted Moses (Num. 11:11–35). In fact, just as the seventy elders were appointed in response to a complaint by Moses to God concerning the burden of leading the nation of Israel, so also were the seven deacons appointed in response to a complaint and the resulting need of the apostles to lighten their burden of overseeing the early Christian church.

The seventy men who assisted Moses were involved in helping him to judge the people, and it also appears, from the story of Ananias and Sapphira, that the apostles were, like Moses, involved in judging the Christian community in Jerusalem. The apostles apparently delegated some of this responsibility to the deacons (Acts 5; Deut. 1:9–17). In Acts, chapter 5, Ananias and Sapphira pledged to the apostles to give a certain sum of the proceeds from the sale of their property to be used in the common distribution. When Ananias and Sapphira kept back some of the money they had promised, Peter confronted them and passed judgment on them. Later on, in Acts 6, the deacons were selected to share in the work of the distribution, which also involved the responsibility of being judges of the people in similar manner to the apostles.

Again, while a good portion of the work of the deacons entailed administrating the material goods and services of the church, their work also included judging the people. In other words, the deacons were spiritual leaders and administrators who helped to relieve some of the responsibilities of the apostles just as the seventy men helped to relieve Moses of some of his responsibilities. The Scriptures show us that Philip and Stephen, two of the seven men who were chosen as deacons, were extraordinary evangelists and important spiritual leaders in the early New Testament church. Furthermore, the qualifications that Paul outlined in 1 Timothy 3:8–13 show that the office of deacon was established to be a function of spiritual leadership and not merely of custodial services. These qualifications also show that this office was reserved only for select men. Let us examine this passage of Scripture below:

> Likewise deacons must be reverent, not double-tongued, not given to much wine, not greedy for money, holding the mystery of the faith with a pure conscience. But let these also first be tested; then let them serve as deacons, being found blameless. Likewise, their wives must be reverent, not slanderers, temperate, faithful in all things. Let deacons be the husbands of one wife, ruling their children and their own houses well. For those who have served well as deacons obtain for themselves a good standing and great boldness in the faith which is in Christ Jesus. (1 Tim. 3:8–13)

Two things are very apparent in this passage of Scripture: (1) deacons should be administrators who are virtuous, judicious, and experienced, and their selection as an administrator in the church should be based largely on their leadership in the home; (2) deacons should be men who "rule" or oversee their household well and they should not have more than one wife. The deaconate is therefore not a non-gendered or generic office in the church, nor does it appear from a biblical perspective that there is a female equivalent office such as "deaconess" in the New Testament. In summary, both the narrative pertaining to the origin of the office of deacon in Acts 6 and the characteristics required for the person who is selected as a deacon in 1 Timothy 3:8–13 support only men serving in this capacity because it involves both spiritual and material governance.

The role and qualifications of elders

We now turn to an examination of the office of elder/bishop from what we find in the narrative of the early New Testament church and in the qualifications highlighted in two of Paul's epistles. In the book of Acts, we may observe that elders are the overseers of the local church or synagogue. There is essentially no change in the responsibility of this office in the transition from the Old Testament to the New Testament. Elders in Moses' day and in the period of the kings were the spiritual overseers of God's people according to tribes and local districts. The elders shared in the responsibility of spiritual leadership along with their principal overseers in the days of Moses, Joshua, and Samuel (Exod. 24:1; Joshua 23:2; 1 Sam. 8:4).

In the times of the kings, the elders continue to be spiritual overseers according to their locality and tribe (1 Kings 8:1). As intimated when discussing the deacons, the task of a spiritual overseer also involved the responsibility of judging. Therefore, elders in both the Old and New Testaments were the principle leaders in settling disputes and in bringing about reconciliation (Ruth 4:9–11; Acts 15). In other words, a significant component of the responsibility of elders is the role that today's secular society has given to judges.

The book of Acts shows that Paul relied on elders to oversee the young churches that he had raised up. Acts 14:23 says of Paul and Barnabas, "So when they had appointed elders in every church, and prayed with fasting, they commended them to the Lord in whom they had believed." Later on, as Paul realized that he would soon go to Rome and suffer a martyr's death, he called for the elders in Ephesus, expressed his love for them and the saints whom they pastored, and admonished them to be faithful overseers: "Therefore take heed to yourselves and to all the flock, among which the Holy Spirit has made you overseers, to shepherd the church of God which He purchased with His own blood" (Acts 20:28).

The passage of Scripture above describes succinctly the responsibility of elders to the local congregation. They are overseers of the "flock," and they should "shepherd the church of God." It is clear from this passage (Acts 20:28) that the work of pastors and elders is essentially the same: they both involve the responsibility of a spiritual overseer and shepherd.

In fact, the apostles at times referred to themselves as elders (1 Peter 5:1; 2 John 1; 3 John 1).

The biblical qualifications for elders are the standard for what is required with respect to serving as a spiritual overseer in the church; whether it is in the office of apostle, elder, or deacon. It seems reasonable to conclude that there are descending degrees of authority from apostleship to eldership to deaconate and also a widening range of leadership influence from deaconate to eldership to apostleship. The apostles' authority and influence seem to be universal while those of the elders and deacons seem to be local. There also appear to have been elders who supervised other elders, as in the cases of Titus and Timothy (Titus 1:4, 5; 1 Tim 1:2, 3).

It is clear from the New Testament that when major disputes needed to be settled, as in the case of the issue of whether Gentile Christians must be circumcised (Acts 15), a council comprising representative elders was to meet with the apostles to reach a decision. The decision of this representative body, composed of both universal (apostles) and local (elders) spiritual overseers, would be the final word on the matter. Be that as it may, what is crystal clear is that each of the offices that we have thus far examined involves spiritual oversight, and, from what we see in the narrative of the early New Testament church, only males were set apart for these specific offices.

We now turn to the qualifications for elder/bishop as stipulated by Paul in his epistle to Timothy and to Titus. The *Seventh-day Adventist Bible Commentary* states: "In apostolic times the office of 'bishop' was the same as that of elder" (vol. 7, p. 297). Accordingly, the term translated "bishop" in 1 Timothy 3:1 (*episkopē*) is equivalent to the term "elder" in Titus 1 (*presbuteros*). In fact, in Titus 1, the terms are used interchangeably (vss. 5, 7). Furthermore, the qualifications that Paul outlined for a bishop in 1 Timothy 3 are virtually the same as the qualifications he set forth for an elder in Titus 1.

> This is a faithful saying: If a man desires the position of a bishop, he desires a good work. A bishop then must be blameless, the husband of one wife, temperate, sober-minded, of good behavior, hospitable, able to teach; not given to wine, not violent, not greedy for money, but gentle, not quarrelsome, not covetous; one who rules his own house well, having his children in submission with all reverence (for if a man does not know how to rule his own house, how

will he take care of the church of God?); not a novice, lest being puffed up with pride he fall into the same condemnation as the devil. Moreover he must have a good testimony among those who are outside, lest he fall into reproach and the snare of the devil. (1 Tim. 3:1–7)

Both the content and the context of 1 Timothy 3 suggest that the offices that Paul describes in this chapter are reserved only for men. Paul states that the bishop should be "the husband of one wife" and "one who rules his own house well." Paul further states, "if a man does not know how to rule his own house, how will he take care of the church of God?" These are clear references both to the male gender and to the responsibility of being an overseer.

In addition, the literal words in the Greek that are used in this passage place emphasis on three specific things: (1) the fact that the qualifications that Paul is referring to pertains to the responsibility of an overseer, (2) that these qualities are mandatory, (3) that the qualifications are not gender-inclusive but can be applied only to males. In Greek, the word translated "bishop," in verse 1, literally means "overseer." The word "must" (*dei* in Greek), in verse 2, denotes an imperative command. Hence, the command that an overseer "*must* be blameless, the husband of one wife" is not optional. The phrase "husband of one wife" is not a gender-inclusive phrase in the original language or in the context of this passage. As Clinton and Gina Wahlen have observed, there are other phrases that Paul could have used if he wanted to include females as well as males in his description. For example, in 1 Timothy 5:9, Paul uses the opposite phrase, "the wife of one man," in reference to widows who are deserving of financial assistance. If his intention were for elders/bishops to include both male and female, he certainly would have made this clear by saying "the husband of one wife or the wife of one husband."[13]

Moreover, 1 Timothy 2 provides the context for chapter 3. In chapter 2, Paul moves from gender-inclusive language in verses 1–7 to gender-specific language in verses 8–15. He moves from talking about praying for all people because it is God's will for all people to be saved to speaking about how godly women should conduct themselves in public, particularly in worship and in public learning environments. After

[13]Clinton and Gina Wahlen, *Women's Ordination: Does it Matter?* (Silver Spring, MD: Bright Shores Publishing, 2015), p. 46.

instructing women to wear modest apparel, in verses 9–10, he states the following in the rest of the chapter:

> Let a woman learn in silence with all submission. And I do not permit a woman to teach or to have authority over a man, but to be in silence. For Adam was formed first, then Eve. And Adam was not deceived, but the woman being deceived, fell into transgression. Nevertheless she will be saved in childbearing if they continue in faith, love, and holiness, with self-control. (1 Tim. 2:11–15)

Before we are tempted to assume that this passage is so clouded with cultural nuances that it is incomprehensible, let us notice three points that are principle-based rather than cultural-based: (1) Paul is addressing the issue of how women should conduct themselves in public; (2) Paul is also addressing the issue of women's submission to male leadership, thereby indicating the issue of women's authority in the presence of men in public worship or in public church related activities; (3) Paul links this issue of women's submission and of their authority in the presence of men to what occurred at Creation in that Adam was created before Eve and was recognize by Eve as the leader of the pair.

On the third point, it is worth briefly mentioning something that I will describe later with more detail. Seventh-day Adventists are accustomed to saying that God gave humanity two institutions in the Garden of Eden at the Creation: the Sabbath and marriage. Let us recognize a third institution: male leadership. When God created Eve from a rib taken out of Adam's side, she came into existence with the consciousness that Adam was the leader of the pair. She also heard Adam define who she was (Gen. 2:23); she heard him define what marriage was (Gen. 2:24); and she understood that, before she was created, Adam had already named and defined all the animals of the earth (Gen. 2:20). The two human beings were equal in terms of their natures, but, just as the Father is the leader of the divine Trinity, so also was Adam the leader of the human pair. In fact, as we will discuss later, marriage is to reflect the kind of equality and voluntary submission to leadership that we observe in the Godhead. But it is not marriage alone that should reflect this divine reality: the church also has a responsibility to reflect the equality, voluntary submission to leadership, and unity of the Godhead (see Ephesians 5).

Let us notice again that the three points mentioned above concerning 1 Timothy 2:11–15 comprise the context that precedes chapter 3:

namely, (1) women's conduct in public, (2) women submission to male leadership, and (3) male leadership authority and women submission as predicated on the Creation narrative. Chapter 3 then deals with the authority of the spiritual overseer in the offices of elder and deacon. Thus, after addressing the issue of women's submission to their husbands' authority in chapter 2, Paul goes on to address male authority as overseers in the offices of elder and deacon. The logical transition between chapters 2 and 3 of First Timothy—from female submission in the presence of male leadership to male leadership as overseers—is critical to being able to understand that, when Paul addresses the qualifications for elders and deacons in chapter 3, he is dealing exclusively with male leadership. Again, chapter 2 helps us to understand that, in chapter 3, Paul is focusing exclusively on male leadership as overseers in the offices of elders and deacons.

Since the context of chapter 2 and the content of chapter 3 of 1 Timothy make it clear that Paul's discussion of the qualifications of elders and deacons pertains to male leadership as overseers in the church, we need not reiterate this as we examine Paul's commentary on the qualifications for elder in his epistle to Titus. However, the first chapter of Titus is quoted below in order to emphasize the importance that Paul attaches to appointing "elders in every city" as spiritual overseers and judges of sound doctrine:

> For this reason I left you in Crete, that you should set in order the things that are lacking, and appoint elders in every city as I commanded you—if a man is blameless, the husband of one wife, having faithful children not accused of dissipation or insubordination. For a bishop must be blameless, as a steward of God, not self-willed, not quick-tempered, not given to wine, not violent, not greedy for money, but hospitable, a lover of what is good, sober-minded, just, holy, self-controlled, holding fast the faithful word as he has been taught, that he may be able, by sound doctrine, both to exhort and convict those who contradict. (Titus 1:5–9)

Paul recognized the importance of ordaining elders in every city where churches had been planted in order to facilitate solid spiritual leadership. Accordingly, he emphasized the qualifications for elders in his letter to Titus. Consistent with Paul's prescription for consecrated men to serve as elders, the narratives of the New Testament show no example of a woman ever being appointed to serve as an elder. Nowhere in the book of Acts or in any of the epistles is there any mention of a woman being set apart as an elder.

Was the authority of prophetesses recognized in the New Testament during the same time that only men were set apart as apostles, elders, and deacons?

The answer to the above question is an unequivocal "yes." The functional authority of female prophets, which primarily entailed providing guidance to God's people, was recognized at the same time that only men were being ordained as apostles, elders, and deacons in the New Testament. At the time of Jesus' birth, Anna—a prophetess whose authority to provide direction to the people of God was unquestioned—prophesied over the infant son of God (Luke 2:36–38). Yet, although Anna's authority as a prophetess is clearly appreciated during this period, there is no evidence that Jesus or the apostles or the elders ordained any woman as an apostle, elder, or deacon.

We may observe two phenomena in both Old and New Testaments: (1) some overseers such as Moses, Samuel, Paul, Peter, and Stephen had the prophetic gift but others did not, and (2) several females, including Miriam, Huldah, Anna, and the four daughters of Philip, either had the prophetic gift or prophesied occasionally but none of them were called or appointed to the position of an overseer (Exod. 15:20; 2 Kings 22:14; Acts 21:8, 9). Miriam, along with Aaron, assisted Moses in leading Israel, but Miriam was never appointed by God, as was Aaron, to help govern the people.

In the case of Deborah, we have an exception that requires some explanation. Deborah was a prophetess, but she also became a judge, which makes her an overseer. However, she temporarily became a judge not by God's appointment but through a default arrangement in which her prophetic guidance was commingled with judging Israel during a time when God allowed heathen nations to oppress Israel because of Israel's disobedience. Prior to the period of the Judges, the nation of Israel was governed by Moses and then by Joshua, along with the assistance of the seventy elders (Exod. 24:1; Num. 11:16). However, during the time of the Judges, Israel was under intermittent oppression and irregular leadership. Accordingly, during the time of Deborah, it was Barak who was supposed to have provided leadership for the oppressed people, but he was not confident in his leadership abilities and thus he constantly relied on Deborah

(Judges, chapters 4, 5). Notwithstanding Barak's reluctance to lead, the narrative of Judges (chapter 4) shows Deborah exhorting Barak to take his rightful place as leader of the chosen people. Thus, Deborah's example as a judge should not be accepted as normative for the people of God. She was an exception to the rule at a time when Israel was under oppression and also had inconsistent leadership.

Miriam and Deborah's example seem to indicate that some women with the prophetic gift provided more than prophetic guidance, for they also collaborated with appointed male leaders in overseeing God's people. However, this is clearly the exception rather than the rule. Ellen White's leadership in our denomination certainly fits the model of the advising prophetess. Miriam, Deborah, and Ellen White were prophetesses whose prophetic gift enabled them to collaborate with chosen male overseers in governing God's people. Yet, none of these women were appointed or ordained to be spiritual overseers in the typical manner that male leaders are.

Does Romans 16:1, 2 indicate that Phoebe was an apostle, elder, or deacon?

Some people have argued that, because Paul recommended Phoebe as a woman worthy of honor for assisting him in the work of the ministry, she was either an apostle, elder, or deacon. However, let us notice in Romans 16:2 that Paul refers to Phoebe as a "helper" (Greek, *prostatis*) not as an apostle, elder, or deacon:

> I commend to you Phoebe our sister, who is a servant of the church in Cenchrea, that you may receive her in the Lord in a manner worthy of the saints, and assist her in whatever business she has need of you; for indeed she has been a *helper* of many and of myself also. (Rom. 16:1, 2, emphasis added)

It appears that Phoebe assisted Paul and others in the same way that a group of women ministered to Jesus out of their substance. There is no indication, on the basis of Romans 16, that Phoebe exercised leadership as an overseer. Some commentators have mistakenly inferred that because the Greek word *diákonos* is used in reference to Phoebe this is an indication that she was a deaconess. However, the word *diákonos* is often used in the New Testament to refer to a servant. For example, in Matthew 20:26–27 Jesus states, "whoever desires to become great among you, let him be your servant (*diákonos*) and whoever desires to be first among you, let him be your slave (*doúlos*)." Also in Mark 9:35 Jesus said to the twelve disciples, "If anyone desires to be first, he shall be last of all and servant (*diákonos*) of all." Accordingly, in Romans 16:1, Phoebe is called a "servant (*diákonos*) of the church in Cenchrea." It is the context that determines whether *diákonos* is used in reference to a servant or to the office of a deacon. The context of Romans 16 does not indicate that Phoebe was a deaconess. Moreover, nowhere in the New Testament is it mentioned that women served in the office of deacon. Phoebe was not called an apostle, an elder, or a deacon. Therefore, we have no basis to assume that Phoebe was an exception to the rule.

Similarly, Aquila and Priscilla, who were husband and wife, became knowledgeable co-laborers with Paul. In fact, 1 Corinthians 16:19 reveals that a church met in their house. While we may assume that Aquila might have been an elder of the church that met in his house, we cannot assume the same for his wife; she was simply his companion or helper in life and ministry. She might even have been supported by the tithes, since she worked along with her husband, although they were self-supporting when they met Paul. However, beyond this, there is no biblical basis from which to extrapolate eldership (see Acts 18:2, 3, 18, 26; Rom. 16:3).

Did God pour out His Spirit on both male and female in the New Testament, in fulfillment of Joel 2:28–30, during the same time that only men were appointed as apostles, elders, and deacons?

The answer to the above question is "yes." In Acts 2:14–21, Peter declared that the outpouring of the Holy Spirit on the day of Pentecost was a fulfillment of the prophecy in Joel chapter 2. One of the predictions in Joel 2, concerning the outpouring of the Holy Spirit, is that the sons and daughters of God's people will prophesy. Acts 21:8, 9 indicates that Philip, the deacon and evangelist, had four daughters who prophesied. Nonetheless, even though the prophetic gift was bestowed on both male and female, only males were appointed to be apostles, elders, and deacons in the early New Testament church. We can glean from this reality that, in both the Old and New Testaments, certain females were called by God to be prophetesses. Yet, this calling did not qualify them to assume the office of a spiritual overseer. The responsibility of being a spiritual overseer was reserved for men. As mentioned above, Miriam and Deborah were exceptional cases.

Yet, even in such cases, these prophetesses were to work as adjuncts to men who were appointed to be the spiritual overseers.

One major mistake that the proponents of women's ordination make is that they equate the role of prophets and prophetesses with the biblical responsibility of being a spiritual overseer. Again, while some overseers also had the gift of prophecy, no prophetess was called or appointed by God to be an overseer on their own. Prophetesses in both the Old and New Testaments consistently played a supportive role to the man appointed to be a spiritual overseer.

Does the concept of "the priesthood of all believers" necessitate women's ordination?

Some proponents of women's ordination argue that the concept of the priesthood of all believers requires that there be no gender barrier concerning who can be ordained as a spiritual overseer in the church. However, this argument reveals a lack of understanding of what the concept of "priesthood of all believers" really means. Christians are a royal priesthood in that we no longer need a human priest to mediate for us, as was the case in the Old Testament. We can go directly to the High Priest, Jesus Christ. 1 Peter 2:9 indicates that believers in Christ have become "a chosen generation, a royal priesthood, a holy nation." But our royal priesthood does not imply that we no longer need spiritual overseers such as apostles, elders, and deacons, nor does it imply that the qualifications for these offices have been changed. We have already seen that, in the New Testament, the office of spiritual overseer is reserved for qualified males. So, although every Christian is automatically a priest as it pertains to access to God without a human mediator, every Christian is not and cannot automatically become an apostle, elder, or deacon.

The great Protestant reformer, Martin Luther, advocated the doctrine of the priesthood of all believers in order to refute the claims of the Roman Catholic hierarchy that the clergy have absolute authority over the people in all spiritual matters. Luther argued that each Christian can go to God directly without the mediation of a priest, interpret the Scriptures on his or her own, and exercise a certain degree of authority in the church. But Luther was not as clear as other reformers in distinguishing the specific authority of those called to be spiritual overseers from the general rights and privileges of believers. Most protestant reformers were in harmony with Luther on the concept of the priesthood of all believers as it pertains to access to God and the right to read and interpret the Scripture on one's own. However, several reformers also emphasized that, while God has commissioned all believers to engage in ministry, most believers are not called to be spiritual overseers.[14]

Was the appointment of apostles, elders, and deacons necessarily based on the gifts of the Spirit in the early New Testament church?

Many supporters of women's ordination argue that women who preach and have certain shepherding qualities should be ordained because their reception of the "pastoral gift" is proof that God has called them to function as an ordained pastor in the church. While this argument sounds plausible, it is nevertheless founded on misguided assumptions. The first problematic assumption is that a spiritual gift is an automatic qualification for any office or role in the church regardless of other qualifications. However, the narratives of Scripture show that, when it comes to the administration of His church, God often calls people to certain roles before they exhibit spiritual gifts related to that particular role. Yet, He equips them with specific gifts once they accept His call.

As an example, the disciple Mathew, was a tax collector when Jesus called him; Peter, James, and John were all fishermen at the time of their calling. The Scriptures do not indicate that these men had any apostolic or pastoral qualities before they were called. Nevertheless, once they accepted Jesus' call, He equipped them to be effective spiritual overseers. Having certain spiritual gifts is, therefore, not a prerequisite for the offices of apostle, elder, and deacon. What is of paramount importance to these offices is the calling of God and the qualifications that have been clearly set forth in Scripture.

Although God equipped prophetesses with gifts similar to those of priests, apostles, and elders, prophetesses did not function as priests, apostles, or elders in the Old and New Testaments. The prophetess remained a mouthpiece for God, not an overseer, except in the unusual case of Deborah. (The same can be said of prophets.)

As mentioned above, in the New Testament, the offices that comprise spiritual overseer are apostles, elders, and deacons. The office that

[14]See Erwin Fahlbusch; Geoffrey William Bromiley, trans., *The Encyclopedia of Christianity* (Grand Rapids, Mich.; Leiden, Netherlands: Wm. B. Eerdmans; Brill, 2005), vol. 4, pp. 350, 351.

Adventists traditionally have called "pastor" or "minister" is essentially that of a supervising elder. While it is possible for women to have a set of qualities given by the Spirit to enable a Christian to effectively provide spiritual care for others, this cannot be construed as a calling to be a spiritual overseer in the manner of apostles, elders, and deacons. Mothers and Sabbath School teachers tend to exhibit pastoral/shepherding gifts within their sphere of influence. However, this is not equivalent to the role of apostles, elders, and deacons.

Chapter 3

Equality and Gender Distinction in Leadership

Is the issue of women's ordination a question of equality?

The topic of women's ordination is primarily a biblical issue. Nevertheless, proponents of women's ordination often accuse those who are opposed to it of endorsing gender discrimination and inequality. They claim that opposing the ordination of women to positions of spiritual leadership in the church is similar to racial discrimination. This argument seems plausible and persuasive on the surface. However, there are many people who are sympathetic to issues of racial and gender discrimination who see the question of women's ordination as essentially a biblical matter. There are clearly times when emerging ideological and cultural mores clash with the requirements of Scripture, as in the case of the legalization of gay marriage in most western societies. We therefore need to establish whether or not the ordination of women to the offices that constitute spiritual overseer in the church is in harmony with Scripture. If the ordination of women is incongruous with the principles and patterns of Scripture and if we deem

Scripture to be in conflict with our notions of equality and justice, then it is incumbent upon us to reexamine these notions.

The conflict between Scripture and popular conceptions of civil rights can be resolved by reconciling our notions of equality with the enduring principles of the Bible. All true knowledge will be in harmony with the principles of God's Word. This means, that rightly understood, both the knowledge we may receive as a result of special revelation (Scripture) and general revelation (nature) are congruent. However, an incorrect comprehension of Scripture may lead people to misunderstand reality. Also, an incorrect understanding of nature may lead to false notions of reality. The Christian church, both Catholic and Protestant, has at times led millions of people astray because it either misinterpreted Scripture or wrongly apprehended nature. In some cases, the church made both errors at the same time.

For example, many Christians believe in the biblically incorrect and illogical doctrine of transubstantiation—the belief that at Communion the bread and the wine become the literal body and blood of Jesus Christ. Moreover, many Christians believe in the unscriptural teaching of the immortality of the soul—the belief that at death the soul lives on forever in either heaven or hell. Transubstantiation is inconsistent with both reason and biblical principles. Likewise, the teaching that the human soul never dies, along with its corollary doctrine of an eternally burning hell, is contrary to both reason and Scripture. Seventh-day Adventists reject transubstantiation and the immortality of the soul primarily on the basis of Scripture. But we also deem them to be inconsistent with the nature of reality.[15] However, long before Adventists rejected the popular doctrine of the immortality of the soul, John Locke, the renowned 17th century philosopher and political theorist, used logic and philosophy to argue that the soul is not immortal.[16] Moreover, Locke, along with many other enlightened thinkers in his day, rejected transubstantiation on the basis of both logic and Scripture.

The point I am making is that, when it comes to the issue of women's ordination and equality, we should expect both the Bible and logic to send a harmonious message. Where there seems to be a conflict, it might very well be as a result of an incorrect grasp of Scripture or faulty reasoning.

---

[15]The very nature of burning requires oxidation and the consumption of that which is burned. That which can die is by definition *not* immortal.

[16]John Locke, "Of Identity and Diversity," in *An Essay Concerning Human Understanding,* Alexander Campbell Fraser, Ed. (New York: Barnes & Noble, 2004, originally published, 1689), pp. 261–278.

As we seek to understand God's will concerning women's ordination and notions of equality, the following questions are worth considering:

Does the Bible reveal a principle of equality that embraces functional distinctions in leadership? Is such a principle consistent with logic and human experience?

The Bible makes it clear that the Son of God and the Father are two separate but equal persons of the Godhead and that they are united in ways that human beings are able to comprehend as well as in ways that transcend our understanding. The Scripture also points to the Son's voluntary submission to the leadership of the Father and the Father's entrusting all things into the care of His Son (John 5:30; 6:39; 3:35). This kind of relationship, where the Son submits to the leadership of the Father and the Father gives all things into the stewardship of the Son, does not appear to have only begun when the Son became incarnate, such a relationship existed prior to the Son's taking on the form of a human being (John 1:1–14).

In John 3:16, Jesus emphasizes the active will of the Father in giving His Son to save the world by using the verb "gave." In verse 17, Jesus again emphasizes the same point by using the verb "send." The Father *gives* the Son and *sends* the Son to save the world. It stands to reason that the Son, who is equal with the Father, cannot be sent or given by the Father to save the world without the Son's consent. In fact, Philippians 2:6, 7 states that the Son "being in the form of God, did not consider it robbery to be equal with God, but made Himself of no reputation, taking the form of a bondservant, and coming in the likeness of men." The Son's submission to the will of the Father is therefore voluntary not mandatory. Moreover, in Revelation 13:8, the Son of God is referred to as "the Lamb slain from the foundation of the world." This means that even before the world was created, it was the Father's will for His Son to be the Lamb of God who takes away the sins of the world. The Son willingly consented and submitted to His Father's will when humanity and planet earth were not even in existence (see Gal. 1:4; 2:20; Eph. 5:25; 1 Tim. 2:6; Titus 2:14; Heb. 9:14).

Based on the above Scriptures, we are compelled to conclude that the Son's submission to the leadership of the Father is not a contradiction to equality. Rather, it reveals an equality that is consistent with the nature of God—an equality in which an equal partner voluntarily submits to the leadership of the other companion while the other partner voluntarily entrusts everything into the submissive companion's care. This kind of divine equality is motivated by love and mutual trust.

Here before us is a picture of divine equality: one that emphasizes leadership-oriented-role distinctions and the principle of voluntary submission. This picture of divine equality and voluntary submission is presented by God to humanity in the Holy Scriptures; it is presented to us not merely for us to reflect on but also for us to emulate. The apostle Paul certainly appreciated this picture of leadership distinctions amid equality: he encouraged Christian families and the church as a body to emulate the divine unity and interdependence manifested in the Godhead.

In 1 Corinthians 12, Paul reminds us that "there are differences of ministries, but the same Lord" (vs. 5) and that "there are diversities of activities, but it is the same God who works all in all" (vs. 6). He then makes an analogy between the church, which is the body of Christ, and the human body. Both the church and the human body have a diversity of members who perform different tasks, but each member of the body must work together under the leadership of the *head* to permit the body to function properly. Accordingly, Paul states:

> And the eye cannot say to the hand, "I have no need of you"; nor again the head to the feet, "I have no need of you." No, much rather, those members of the body which seem to be weaker are necessary. And those members of the body which we think to be less honorable, on these we bestow greater honor; and our unpresentable parts have greater modesty, but our presentable parts have no need. But God composed the body, having given greater honor to that part which lacks it, that there should be no schism in the body, but that the members should have the same care for one another. And if one member suffers, all the members suffer with it; or if one member is honored, all the members rejoice with it. Now you are the body of Christ, and members individually. (1 Cor. 12: 21–27)

In his analogy of the church and the human body, Paul reminds us that what appears to be inequality between the members of the body was designed by God so that there would be mutual care and trust and an overall unity in the body. While all the members of the church cannot hold the most prestigious or authoritative office, all the members should work and care for each other so that there is unity and not division.

Paul ends chapter 12 of 1 Corinthians by declaring in verse 31: "And yet I show you a more excellent way." Here he is referring to the point that all the members of the church should see to it that their actions and desires are motivated by love. This is the point he explains in poetic language in chapter 13, which is commonly dubbed "the love chapter." Rather than seeking after the highest office, we should be content with the gifts and positions that God has entrusted to us and be committed to minister out of pure love.

> *In his analogy of the church and the human body, Paul reminds us that what appears to be inequality between the members of the body was designed by God so that there would be mutual care and trust and an overall unity in the body.*

The apostle Paul is even more explicit in addressing role distinction and equality when he deals with the distinction between men and women in regard to authority and leadership. He shows that there is a universal principle of headship in leadership where men are the head of women just as God the Father is the head of the Son. In 1 Corinthians 11:3, Paul states, "But I want you to know that the head of every man is Christ, the head of woman is man, and the head of Christ is God." This is clearly not a reference to the salvation or respective worth of male or female human beings. When it comes to salvation or existential worth, "there is neither male nor female" for we "are all one in Christ Jesus" (Gal. 3:28). Each human being, irrespective of gender, has equal worth in Christ. However, with respect to leadership authority, the male is the leader of the female just as the Father is the leader of the Godhead.

Although 1 Corinthians 11:3 has references to cultural customs such as head coverings, the principle of male leadership authority is as clear as the principle that the seventh day is the Sabbath in the fourth commandment (Exod. 20:8–11), though it too has references to cultural elements such as regulations regarding livestock. Moreover, just as the seventh-day Sabbath of the fourth commandment is rooted in the Creation, so also is the principle of male headship. Notice that Paul makes an explicit connection to the Creation when talking about the principle of male leadership. In verses 8–10 of 1 Corinthians 11, he states explicitly why men are the leaders of women, "For man is not from woman, but woman from man. Nor was man created for the woman, but woman for the man. For this reason the woman ought to have a symbol of authority on her head, because of the angels."

As mentioned, Paul links this same principle of male leadership to the Creation in 1 Timothy when he discusses how women should conduct themselves in the presence of men in worship. In 1 Timothy 2:12–14, Paul states, "And I do not permit a woman to teach or to have authority over a man, but to be in silence. For Adam was formed first, then Eve. And Adam was not deceived, but the woman being deceived, fell into transgression."

The sequence of Adam and Eve's creation clearly reveals who was the leader of the pair. Adam was created first. He also named the animals according to their distinct characteristics before Eve was created (Gen. 2:20–22). When God created Eve from a rib taken from Adam's side and presented her to her husband, her husband named her according to her relation to the male gender. He declared in Genesis 2:23, "This is now bone of my bones and flesh of my flesh; she shall be called Woman [*ishah*], because she was taken out of Man [*ish*]." There is no doubt that Eve recognized Adam as the leader of their pair. There is no question that she understood that she was his equal in terms of her existence as a human being, but it was clear to her that she was designed by God to be his "helper" (Gen. 2:20).

As we reflect on the narrative of Adam and Eve at the Fall in Genesis 3, we recall the words of Paul in 1 Timothy 2:14, "For Adam was formed first, then Eve. And Adam was not deceived, but the woman being deceived, fell into transgression." Let us notice that even though Eve was deceived and fell into transgression first, God confronted Adam first before speaking a word to Eve. The reason why God required Adam to account for his actions first was because Adam was the leader of the pair. The emphasis on Adam's leadership is even more explicit when God pronounced punishment upon him. God declared, "Because you have **heeded the voice of your wife**, and have eaten from the tree of which I commanded you saying, 'You shall not eat of it': 'Cursed is the ground for your sake; in toil you shall eat of it all the days of your life." (Gen. 3:17, emphasis supplied)

When Adam "heeded the voice" of his wife in doing wrong, he neglected to faithfully fulfill the leadership role that God designed for him. Ironically, his wife was leading him into doing wrong rather than he, the divinely designated leader, was leading her in doing what is right. Consequently, when God pronounced punishment on Eve, He predicted that, as a result of sin, there will be a genetic propensity in wives to rival

the leadership of their husbands and that there will also be a genetic pre-
disposition in husbands to rule over their wives: "Your desire shall be for
your husband, and he shall rule over you" (Gen. 3:16). The phrase, "your
desire shall be for your husband," implies that the wife will be tempted to
challenge the leadership of her husband. The word "rule" in Bible times
does not always have the negative connotation that modern society associ-
ates with it; its sense depends on the context in which it is used. However,
in this context, "rule" implies that the husband would be tempted to dominate his wife.

The apostle Paul, keenly aware of the hereditary penchant in the
female to rival the leadership of the male and the proclivity of the male to
rule over the female, admonishes Christian husbands and wives to behave
differently. In Ephesians 5, Paul tells husbands to love their wives rather
than to rule over them and he tells wives to submit to the leadership of
their husbands rather than to challenge them.

> Wives, submit to your own husbands, as to the Lord. For the hus-
> band is head of the wife, as also Christ is head of the church; and
> He is the Savior of the body. Therefore, just as the church is subject
> to Christ, so let the wives be to their own husbands in everything.
> Husbands, love your wives, just as Christ also loved the church and
> gave Himself for it. (Eph. 5:22–25)

Paul is explicit in emphasizing the extent to which the husband should
go to love his wife: he is to love his wife as Christ loved the church and
gave Himself for it. This is an emphasis on love-motivated servant leadership on the part of the husband. Paul is also explicit in highlighting
the extent to which the wife should go to submit to the leadership of
her husband: she is to submit to him in everything as the church is subject to Christ. This is a reflection of the model of love and submission
that is manifested in the Godhead: the Son submits to the leadership
of the Father in everything, and the Father loves the Son so much that
He entrusts everything into His care. What appears to be inequality in
the roles of the male and female in marriage is in reality not a product
of sin but the very design of God before the foundations of the world in
order that in marriage humanity might reflect the love and mutual trust
that exist in the Godhead. Likewise, what appears to be inequality in
the church, in that the highest leadership roles are reserved for men, is
in reality designed by God to enable the church to reflect the love and
mutual trust that exist in the Godhead.

Now, it is understandable that a wife would not submit to any immoral behavior required by a wicked husband because she must first submit to the will of Christ. However, the reality that many marriages do not reflect the ideal of what God designed marriage to be does not negate the validity or urgency of obeying God's precepts concerning marriage. Nor does the reality that the Christian church has, in many cases, misrepresented what God has enjoined regarding leadership, equality, and mutual trust, negate the binding nature of His principles.

In many ways, the church is to function as a large family in which the following dynamics are in operation: oversight is reserved for select men, voluntary submission to spiritual overseers is respectfully exhibited by both men and women, men demonstrate loving servant leadership, women lead in supportive roles, and wives are submissive to their husbands. In the home, children should obey their parents and fathers should not provoke their children. Likewise, in the church, the entire congregation should submit to the leadership of their male spiritual overseers, and these servant leaders should love rather than dominate those who are in subjection to them.

As we have seen, what we have in Scripture is a fairly clear picture of the issue of equality and leadership distinctions. In the Bible we have a paradigm of leadership and gender distinctions that embraces a concept of equality that includes voluntary submission. This paradigm is both reasonable and conducive to human experience. Where the biblical principle of leadership distinction and loving service is being practiced at home and in the church, a beautiful harmony and powerful testimony redound to the glory of God. The Christian church, therefore, has a choice to make with respect to whether it allows God's Word to shape its view of equality or adheres to society's conceptions of equality.

Some Christians claim that women's ordination is a sign of progress. However, in light of what we have studied above, women's ordination is actually an accommodation to society's view of progress and equality. The ordination of women is not genuinely a step forward but a step backward in order to accommodate society's standards. While it is not my intention to equate women's ordination with polygamy, I would like to emphasize that God did not condone polygamy when Abraham and his descendants accommodated the cultural mores of their time. In those days, God winked at the ignorance of His people. But Christians today have been given greater light and are thus accountable to maintain monogamy. Likewise, I believe that God winks at attempts to install women pastors and elders in His church because in many cases this has been done out of a lack of understanding of Scripture. However, the Lord is calling His church to walk in the light of His Word and in the example set before us by His Son, Jesus Christ.

According to Daniel 12, the saints who are living in the time of the end will become wiser, purified, and shine like the stars while the ungodly will become more wicked and will not understand the gravity or urgency of the time of the end. There are some in our church who view "progress" as essentially keeping up with society, but this is not progress; rather, it is regression and conformity to the world. The saints in the time of the end will not be moving backwards into worldly conformity but forward into wisdom and obedience of every word that proceeds out of the mouth of God.

Does Galatians 3:28 indicate that believers are equal in regard to leadership roles?

The most frequently quoted verse of Scripture among those who support women's ordination is the following: "There is neither Jew nor Greek, there is neither slave nor free, there is neither male nor female; for you are all one in Christ Jesus" (Gal. 3:28). The immediate context of this verse indicates that Paul is talking about justification through Jesus Christ as opposed to the law. Paul's message is that whoever accept Jesus Christ by faith receives salvation regardless of race, ethnicity, social standing, or gender. All believers are equally justified by Christ. This passage of Scripture has nothing to do with leadership roles in the church. Notice that the immediate context, verses 24–27, is crystal clear about the fact that the focus is justification by faith. Accordingly, verse 24 states, "Therefore the law was our tutor to bring us to Christ, that we might be justified by faith."

In other places in Scripture, Paul used similar language to that which is found in Galatians 3:28 when describing the inclusiveness of salvation and the accompanying membership in the body of Christ, the church. For example, in Colossians 3:9–11, he states the following:

> "Do not lie to one another, since you have put off the old man with his deeds, and have put on the new man who is renewed in knowledge according to the image of Him who created him, where there is neither Greek nor Jew, circumcised nor uncircumcised, barbarian, Scythian, slave nor free, but Christ is all and in all."

The passage of Scripture above shows that human beings have equal access to salvation, and all can enjoy membership in the church through

Christ. There is no merit with respect to race, ethnicity, social status, or anything else because Christ's justification and sanctification make each believer a new person and gives the believer a standing before God that is similar to that of Adam and Eve before the Fall.

In 1 Corinthians 12, Paul provides a description of unity amid diversity of spiritual gifts and leadership roles among believers who are equal in Christ regarding salvation and membership in the church. Notice that, in verse 13, Paul used similar words as in Galatians 3:28 in arguing that all who accept Jesus as Savior become equal as members of the body of Christ regardless of such things as ethnicity or social status: "For by one Spirit we were all baptized into one body—whether Jews or Greeks, whether slaves or free—and have all been made to drink into one Spirit." Moreover, Paul is clear, in 1 Corinthians 12, that there is a beautiful diversity of gifts and that there are different levels of leadership in the church. Notice, for example, verses 28: "And God has appointed these in the church: first apostles, second prophets, third teachers, after that miracles, then gifts of healings, helps, administrations, varieties of tongues." Again, Paul's message is that believers are equal and united through the Holy Spirit as members of the body of Christ but that there is also diversity of gifts and levels of leadership in the body—the church. In other words, the equality of Christians in terms of salvation and membership in the church does not negate God-ordained levels of leadership or the headship principle.

Why did God strike Miriam with leprosy?

Although Aaron and Miriam both spoke grudgingly against the leadership of Moses, only Miriam was afflicted with leprosy. On the surface, this seems unfair, but, when we perceive what really led Aaron and Miriam to utter disparaging statements against Moses' leadership, we begin to understand why Miriam suffered this punishment. Numbers 11 shows the context that preceded God's sentence on Miriam, and the punishment itself is recorded in Numbers 12. In Numbers 11:16–35, we may trace some very interesting events concerning leadership functions and Miriam's coveting of the office of overseer.

First, let us notice that, in response to Moses' complaint concerning bearing alone the burden of leading the nation of Israel, God directed Moses to appoint seventy male elders to help him govern the people. Furthermore, the Lord gave all seventy elders the Spirit that was upon

Moses so that they would have wisdom and meekness like Moses in lead-ing the people. As a result of the Spirit's descent upon the seventy elders, they all prophesied, "although they never did so again" (Num. 11:25). Even though the Bible is not explicit on the matter, we may infer that Miriam, the prophetess, and Aaron, the priest, were not happy about the delegation of authority to the seventy elders. Miriam and Aaron felt that, as Moses' older siblings and as leaders endowed with special gifts, they should be the only ones helping Moses to oversee the people, not the seventy elders. This is the begin-ning of their feeling slighted and of their subsequent murmurings, which led them, in chapter 12, to complain against the non-Hebrew ethnicity of Moses' wife and to undermine Moses' leadership.

But let us ask again, why did God punish Miriam with leprosy and not Aaron? The fact that the Bible does not mention Aaron's punishment but only Miriam's probably serves to highlight the reality that Miriam's sin is greater than Aaron's. As a prophetess, Miriam's responsibility was to exhort the people to follow Moses' leadership; God did not call her, as He did the seventy male elders and Aaron, to the respon-sibility of being an overseer of the nation of Israel. However, in her role as prophetess, she was permit-ted to work along with Aaron and

> *Again, both Miriam and Aaron sinned in envying Moses' position, complaining against him and undermining his leadership, but Miriam's sin involved something more grievous in the sight of God: not merely coveting Moses' position, but coveting, just like Lucifer, a position that God did not create her to fulfill.*

Moses in governing God's people. She was to be a helper in leadership, not an overseer on her own. At its core, Miriam's sin was that she was coveting a role to which God did not call females. Again, both Miriam and Aaron sinned in envying Moses' position, complaining against him and undermining his leadership, but Miriam's sin involved something more grievous in the sight of God: not merely coveting Moses' position, but coveting, just like Lucifer, a position that God did not create her to fulfill.

What guidance does Scripture provide concerning the role and leadership of women in the church?

As we have observed, the Bible shows a pattern and a principle of male leadership with respect to serving as a spiritual overseer in the roles of priests, judges, apostles, elders, and deacons. However, this does not mean that Scripture excludes the involvement and leadership of women in other ministry roles. Women have been used by God throughout the ages to educate children, assist men in spiritual leadership, and to extend healing and compassion to others. Among the notable roles for women's leadership, as highlighted in Scripture, is prophetess (Exod. 15:20; 2 Kings 22:14; Luke 2:36), mother (1 Sam. 1:22, 23; Luke 1:26–60), steward of the home (Prov. 31:13–24), healthcare worker (Exod. 1:17; 2:7), caretaker/community service agent (Luke 8:2, 3; Mark 15:40, 41; Acts 9:36, 39), mentor of other women (Titus 2:3–5), and assistant to male spiritual overseers (Exod. 15:20; Acts 18:26).

Thus, it can be observed from Scripture that it is God's will for women to be involved in various ministries and roles in the church. In the offices that constitute a spiritual overseer (e.g., apostle, elder, and deacon), only men should lead. However, it is permissible for a woman to function as an assistant to a male spiritual overseer, as can be seen in the case of Miriam with Moses and of Priscilla with Aquila (Exod. 15:20; Acts 18:26). As mentioned in the previous chapter, the ministry of Deborah is an exception to the rule, for, while she was called to be a prophetess, she also functioned as a "judge" because of Barak's reluctance to fulfill his role of leadership.

Chapter 4

Answering Popular Claims About Women's Ordination

In the previous chapters, we established that there is strong biblical support for not ordaining women to offices that constitute a spiritual overseer. Also, we saw that the Bible has a model of leadership that entails the voluntary submission of the Son to the Father, the voluntary submission of the wife to the husband, and the voluntary submission of both men and women to male spiritual overseers. In this chapter, we will answer four popular claims about women's ordination. These claims are posed in the form of questions below.

Is the claim that the Bible does not explicitly forbid ordaining women a sound basis upon which to build an argument in favor of women's ordination?

The above question can be easily answered when we observe that, as in the case of women's ordination, the Bible does not explicitly forbid the observance of Sunday as a day of worship in honor of Christ's resurrection. We know that the Bible clearly requires human beings to observe the seventh-day Sabbath by abstaining from work and business to be able to focus on worshipping the Creator. Yet, again, there is no Scripture that forbids observing Sunday as a day of worship. However, it is clear to us that, if we should observe Sunday as a day of worship in addition to or instead of the Sabbath, we would be undermining the distinctiveness of the seventh-day Sabbath and also adding a human tradition to the clear commandment of God. Likewise, we have discovered that the Bible consistently reserves ordination for men who are appointed or elected to serve as spiritual overseers. Therefore, if we should ordain women to serve as pastors, elders, or deacons, we would be undermining the distinctiveness of what God has enjoined. We would also be adding our traditions to the clear requirements of the Lord.

Important matters such as God's requirements concerning worship or leadership should not be decided on the basis of what God has not forbidden but rather on the basis of what God has prescribed. Jesus, our perfect example, demonstrated in His training and leadership of the twelve apostles that it is God's will for select males to serve as spiritual overseers in His church and Paul clearly articulated in his description of the qualifications for elders and deacons that male spiritual overseers is what God has prescribed for His church.

When the church takes the time to deal with a controversial issue, does this necessarily result in the church becoming distracted from its primary mission?

Leading voices on both sides of the women's ordination question seem to agree on the argument that the women's ordination debate has and will distract the church from its mission. However, the world church, under the leadership of Pastor Ted Wilson, has been dealing with the issue of women's ordination while being very focused on important aspects of the church's mission such as evangelizing the world's largest cities, facilitating revival and reformation, empowering young people to minister for Christ, and providing encouragement to self-supporting ministries and total member involvement. Even with the debate, the world church has not been distracted from its mission.

However, due to the fact that the Seventh-day Adventist Church has not dealt with women's ordination in a comprehensive manner and due to inconsistent policies in the church regarding the ordination of women (such as ordaining women as elders but not as pastors), the issue of ordination has been a major threat to the unity of the world church. Thus, while the world church has successfully maintained focus on its mission, it is nevertheless in jeopardy of being fragmented by the incessant conflicts and independent actions of unions and divisions in regard to women's ordination.

While the world church has successfully maintained focus on its mission, it is nevertheless in jeopardy of being fragmented by the incessant conflicts and independent actions of unions and divisions in regard to women's ordination.

As has already been mentioned, when the apostles and elders in the early New Testament church gathered to deal with the issue of whether or not Gentile Christians should be circumcised, they thoroughly dealt with the issue on the basis of the harmony between Scripture and the providential leadings of the Holy Spirit. Their decision was not made on the basis of political or cultural expedience or out of fear that the church would be divided. Thus, when they took the time to deal comprehensively with this controversial matter, it resulted in the progress of the Great Gospel Commission and the continued unity of the church.

Is there merit to the claim that different opinions on women's ordination among Bible scholars is evidence that the Bible is not clear on the subject?

Supporters of women's ordination argue that divergent views of Adventist theologians on this topic is an indication that the Bible is not clear on the subject. Thus, if the Bible is unclear on the matter, then the church should not disapprove of the ordaining of women to the gospel ministry. If the Scriptures were genuinely unclear or agnostic on this subject then I would agree that the church should not refuse ordination to women. However, the fact that Bible scholars do not agree on this topic is not evidence that Scripture is unclear about it. Scores of theologians do not agree with Adventists and other Sabbatarians that God requires humanity to observe the seventh-day Sabbath, instead of the first day of the week, as a day of worship, yet the Bible is clear on this subject.

During the mid-19th century, there were robust debates on various points of doctrine among Adventist pioneers as they sought to understand the fundamental beliefs of their faith. However, the church leaders came together in Bible conferences to pray, study, and deliberate on these issues. There were times, in some of these Bible conferences, when it was not clear to the participants which way to go; nevertheless, they persevered in prayer and Bible study, and they waited for guidance from God. The following quotation represents one of two graphic descriptions by the Adventist pioneer and prophetess, Ellen G. White, concerning how our leaders actively waited on the Lord when they could not see clearly what position to take:

> Often we remained together until late at night, and sometimes through the entire night, praying for light and studying the Word. Again and again these brethren came together to study the Bible, in order that they might know its meaning, and be prepared to teach it with power. When they came to the point in their study where they said, 'We can do nothing more,' the Spirit of the Lord would come upon me, I would be taken off in vision, and a clear explanation of the passages we had been studying would be given me, with instruction as to how we were to labor and teach effectively. Thus light was given that helped us to understand the scriptures in regard to Christ, His mission, and His priesthood. A line of truth extending from that time to the time when we shall enter the city of God, was made plain to me, and I gave to others the instruction that the Lord had given me.[17]

God will grant His church understanding of the women's ordination issue when we follow the example of our pioneers highlighted above. Divergent perspectives on this controversial issue is not a good reason for us to conclude that the matter is obscure in the Bible. We should rather prayerfully search the Scriptures like those who dig deep in search of rare stones and metals.

Is the practice of ordination unbiblical?

It has become customary now for the women's ordination movement among Adventists to assert that ordination itself is unbiblical and that it

---

[17]Ellen G. White, *Early Writings* (Hagerstown, MD: Review and Herald Publishing, 1945), pp. xxii, xxiii, taken from "Testimonies for the Church Containing Letters to Physicians and Ministers Instruction to Seventh-day Adventists" [SpTB02] (1904), pp. 56, 57.

is derived from Roman Catholic theology and practice. However, this is a mere rhetorical distraction, yes, a smoke screen. The fact is that the concept of setting apart spiritual overseers as apostles, elders, and deacons by prayer and laying on of hands is clearly set forth in the Bible. For example, the Gospel of Mark says of Jesus, "Then He appointed twelve, that they might be with Him and that He might send them out to preach" (Mark 3:14). In addition, Acts 6:6 describes the ordination of the deacons in the following way: "whom they set before the apostles and when they had prayed they laid hands on them." Whether or not the terms "ordain" and "ordination" are used in Scripture is of no real consequence to the reality that apostles, elders, and deacons were set apart for their sacred responsibilities as spiritual overseers. The practice of setting apart spiritual overseers by praying and the laying of hands is what we today refer to as ordination. This practice is clearly biblical, whether or not the term "ordination" is the correct word to describe it and regardless of the fact that the Roman Catholic Church ascribes to the concept of ordination its own theology and tradition.

Chapter 5

Relevant Contemporary Issues

Today's society finds itself reactively seeking to avoid some of the abuses emanating from certain traditional beliefs and practices. In this predicament, many people tend to opt for leniency, relativism, and pluralism out of fear of repeating the mistakes of the past. The Seventh-day Adventist Church, as a part of society, is not unsympathetic to the sentiments of the culture in which it exists. However, it desires to be faithful to God. For example, many Adventists sense that they need to be more loving and less judgmental, but they also recognize that they would be unfaithful to God if they were to embrace a permissive and relativistic lifestyle. In this context, the women's ordination debate has exposed other contemporary issues that are of paramount importance to the Seventh-day Adventist Church, such as biblical authority, hermeneutics, homosexuality, and abortion. In this chapter, we examine how biblical authority and hermeneutics are essential to a proper understanding of women's ordination, homosexuality, and abortion.

Biblical authority and hermeneutics

The question of how authoritative the Bible should be in the life of a believer has a tremendous impact on what notions the believer is willing to embrace. In addition, the conclusions and positions of most believers tend to be influenced by their particular interpretation of certain biblical passages. As mentioned, hermeneutics refer to methods of interpreting Scripture. Seventh-day Adventists reject the historical-critical method of Bible interpretation because it presupposes that the Scriptures are merely the product of a community of religious people with biases, and, therefore, the Scriptures should be subjected to ideologically laden analyses that have been used on other ancient documents: namely, source criticism, form criticism, tradition criticism, and redaction criticism. Adventists use the method of Bible interpretation that most of the sixteenth century Protestant reformers used because it respects the divine-human origin of Scripture. This is the "historical-grammatical" method. The historical-grammatical method seeks to understand the context of a passage of Scripture and the meaning of the Bible as a whole by examining such things as authorship, language, date of composition, and historical background. However, it does not force upon the meaning of Scripture extraneous ideas from naturalism or the social sciences, as is the case with the historical-critical method.

Based on the historical-grammatical method and insights from Ellen G. White, the Seventh-day Adventist Church embraces certain presuppositions and methods. The following is a summary of these:

1. In the production of the Old and New Testaments, God inspired and guided select human beings at various times and from a variety of backgrounds to write His thoughts in their own words and within the limits of human language. The inspired writers were God's instruments, yet God remained the author; thus, the message of Scripture is the Word of God.

2. The Bible is the authoritative revelation of divine truths, which have universal application to humanity. The truths revealed in Scripture are not limited to spiritual matters; rather, they are universal and absolute. Hence, the historical, genealogical, and geographical data presented in the Bible are reliable. When rightly interpreted, facts and evidence from the study of nature and human interaction will be in harmony with the truths derived from Scripture.

3. There is a unity within the entire Bible; this unity may be observed between the Old and New Testaments and within each Testament.

4. The Scriptures should be taken literally and understood as they were originally presented unless the context indicates otherwise.

Accordingly, the historical context and the literary-grammatical construction should be analyzed. More specifically, the context of the words, the literary form, the thought, the chapter, the book, and the entire canon should be considered.

5. The Bible provides keys to unlock its own interpretation; therefore, its meaning should not be determined by external sources such as tradition, science, philosophy, or culture.
6. The ultimate goal of studying Scripture is to understand the total truths of the entire Bible so we may do all of God's will and may strengthen our relationship with Him.
7. In order to properly understand Scripture, we need to depend on the illumination of the One who inspired the Bible writers, the Holy Spirit.[18]

As a result of using the historical-grammatical method, Adventists have discovered several themes and principles embedded in Scripture. For example, two pervasive motifs throughout the Bible are: (1) The great controversy between God and Satan, which began in heaven with the rebellion of Lucifer and which unfolds on earth among human beings until the final judgment, and (2) the salvation and restoration of human beings by the Son of God. Closely related to these motifs is the principle that the order, structure, and institutions that God established for humanity at Creation represent the foundations upon which society should operate. Hence, the fall of Adam and Eve and the entrance of sin into the world do not alter God's expectation that human beings should observe the institutions of marriage, the Sabbath, and the headship/leadership role of men in exactly the way He originally established them. While God extends mercy and forbearance on human failings, as in the case of permitting divorce under certain circumstances (Deut. 24:1–4; Ezra 10:16–19; Matt. 19:3–12; 1 Cor. 7:10–15), He forbids any reversal of the original creative order, as in the cases of same-sex cohabitation and human-animal cohabitation (Lev. 18:22, 23; Rom. 1:26, 27), the observance of the first day of the week instead of the seventh day as the Sabbath (Exod. 20:8–11), and the reversal of the headship role given to men (1 Tim. 2:12–14; Eph. 5:22–25).

The way Adventists explain the Seventh-day Sabbath is an excellent example of how to apply the historical-grammatical method to a subject that is controversial in the Christian world but that is clearly addressed in

---

[18]See Gerhard F. Hasel, *Biblical Interpretation Today* (Washington, D.C: Biblical Research Institute, 1985); "Method of Bible Study," Seventh-day Adventist Church, Oct. 12, 1986, retrieved from https://1ref.us/1cv, accessed 8/20/20.

Scripture. Adventists believe in the seventh-day Sabbath on the basis of the full authority of the Scriptures and of proper hermeneutics. Therefore, Adventists observe the Sabbath from sunset Friday to sunset Saturday in spite of the fact that the vast majority of Christians around the world observe Sunday in honor of Jesus' resurrection. Christians who observe Sunday do not have any substantive biblical passage to support their position. Rather, they argue that the seventh-day Sabbath was relegated to the Jewish people and the law and that Jesus has freed us from the law and placed us under grace and, therefore, Christians honor Jesus when they observe the same day that He rose from the grave.

The way Adventists explain the Seventh-day Sabbath is an excellent example of how to apply the historical-grammatical method to a subject that is controversial in the Christian world but that is clearly addressed in Scripture.

In reply to this argument, Adventists emphasize that God established the seventh-day Sabbath at Creation before the Fall and before the nation of Israel came into existence. Furthermore, while the Jewish ceremonial law is not binding upon Christians, Jesus commanded His followers to observe the moral law as codified in the Ten Commandments. In the fourth commandment, God explicitly commanded humanity to remember the Sabbath to keep it holy by abstaining from work on the seventh day of the week. However, there is no scripture that commands us to observe the first day of the week in honor of Christ's resurrection. Moreover, the New Testament shows that both Jesus and the apostles observed the seventh-day Sabbath.

The Adventist argument in favor of the seventh-day Sabbath is based entirely on Scripture, not on tradition, as is the case of the observance of the first day of the week in honor of Jesus' resurrection. Using proper hermeneutics, Adventists carefully show that the seventh-day Sabbath, derived from the Creation and the fourth commandment, should be distinguished from the ceremonial sabbaths that consisted of feast days such as Passover, the Feast of Tabernacles, and Pentecost. Thus, on the basis of the historical-grammatical method of interpretation, Adventists have been able to clearly separate the local cultural elements relating to the ceremonies of the nation of Israel from the universal principles concerning the seventh-day Sabbath.

Adventists are viewed by other denominations as peculiar because of our support of the seventh-day Sabbath and our teachings concerning the perpetuity of the moral law, the state of the dead, the pre-advent judgment and the sanctuary, and health reform. Yet, no church or denomination has been able to successfully argue that Adventists are not following Scripture in their espousal of these beliefs. Thus, the adherence to the full authority of Scripture and to proper hermeneutics has enabled the Seventh-day Adventist Church to eschew many of the popular unbiblical notions, derived from tradition, that have crept into Christianity.

Women's ordination and hermeneutics

While Adventists do not subscribe to the historical-critical method of Bible interpretation, the progressive deconstructionist movement within Adventism has been selectively borrowing and propagating some of the presuppositions and arguments of this method. For example, the progressive deconstructionists will argue that 1 Timothy 2:11–14 is a culturally conditioned passage of Scripture, and that its meaning should, therefore, not be taken literally or normatively. However, as I have shown in a previous chapter, Paul supports his argument that women should not have authority over man in public worship by appealing to the fact that Adam was created first. This is the immediate context of the passage of Scripture. One of the interpretive procedures highlighted by the Seventh-day Adventist Church in its 1986 "Method of Bible Study" is encapsulated in the following words: "Study the context of the passage under consideration by relating it to the sentences and paragraphs immediately preceding and following it. Try to relate the ideas of the passage to the line of thought of the entire Bible book."[19]

Those who claim that 1 Timothy 2:11–14 is culturally conditioned and cannot be cited for support against women's ordination are certainly not following the foregoing method of Bible study. The culturally conditioned argument creates a void of uncertainty that allows people to fill in the gap with their own ideologically slanted interpretation. However, Paul's appeal to the order established at the Creation in which Adam was formed first and recognized by Eve as the leader of the pair, provides a key to unlocking the meaning of 1 Timothy 2:11–14.

---

[19]"Methods of Bible Study," Oct. 12, 1986, retrieved from https://1ref.us/1cv, accessed 8/20/20.

Unfortunately, when confronted with difficult passages that do not support their ideological positions, some believers have resorted to the flawed allegorical method that was popular during medieval times. This method subjectively subjugates the literal sense of a passage of Scripture to the so-called "spiritual sense." It superimposes opinions that are not found in the passage of Scripture upon the text. By the way, the allegorical method allows the Roman Catholic Church to influence the meaning of Scripture by appealing to the Catholic Church's other sources of authority: namely, sacred traditions and the teaching authority of the Church. In other words, the spiritual sense is forced onto a biblical passage through the lenses of sacred tradition and the teaching authority of the Roman Catholic Church.[20]

The consequences of following Roman Catholicism in allegorizing difficult passages of Scripture would certainly prove fatal to the beliefs of Adventism. Nevertheless, progressive deconstructionist Adventists have applied this method selectively in their interpretation of certain passages of Scripture. As an example, the progressive deconstructionists uproot Galatians 3:28 from its immediate context and apply it in an allegorical manner to their argument. Galatians 3:28 states, "There is neither Jew nor Greek, there is neither slave nor free, there is neither male nor female; for you are all one in Christ Jesus." As we saw in Chapter 3, this text clearly refers to the equality of believers regarding salvation and membership in the body of Christ. The text has nothing to say about leadership roles. However, in the deconstructionists' view, the literal sense

> *The consequences of following Roman Catholicism in allegorizing difficult passages of Scripture would certainly prove fatal to the beliefs of Adventism. In some ways similar to both the allegorical method and the historical-critical method, the "principle-based, historical-cultural" approach allows for subjective interpretation of passages of Scripture that are deem to be culturally conditioned.*

---

[20]Gerhard F. Hasel, *Biblical Interpretation Today* (Washington, D.C: Biblical Research Institute, 1985).

is supplanted by a "spiritual sense" that opens all levels of leadership to believers without regard to gender.[21]

Given the tendency of progressive deconstructionists to selectively lean towards the old allegorical method and the culturally conditioned argument, it is no surprise that the current NAD leadership gravitates toward a different method of interpretation than what Adventists have relied on for approximately 170 years. As mentioned, the Seventh-day Adventist Church has been using the historical-grammatical method throughout our existence as a church. However, the current NAD leadership signaled in its "Theology of Ordination Study Committee Report" at its 2013 year-end meeting that it prefers the "principle-based, historical-cultural" method.[22] In some ways similar to both the allegorical method and the historical-critical method, the "principle-based, historical-cultural" approach allows for subjective interpretation of passages of Scripture that are deem to be culturally conditioned.

Homosexuality and biblical authority

The vast majority of Seventh-day Adventists around the world believe that homosexuality is condemned in very strong terms in the Bible. However, as society in the twenty-first century has become more accepting of homosexual relationships, a growing segment of Adventists have adopted an accommodationist approach to the LGBT community that is fraught with ambivalence and ambiguity. Most Adventists agree that the church should find ways to minister to the LGBT community, but they are major differences in approach. For example, the majority of Adventists believe that, while the church should be sensitive to the needs and struggles of the LGBT community, LGBT persons must be transformed before holding membership and office in the church. The majority of Adventists also believe that the homosexual lifestyle can be prevented. However, most members who identify themselves as progressive Adventists tend to fall into one of the following three categories: (1) those who believe that the church should do more to accommodate the LGBT community but who are unclear as to where to draw the line in terms of accepting them into membership and allowing them to hold

---

[21]See "GC TOSC Committee, Women's Ordination- A North American Division Report," Jan. 21, 2014, p. 12, retrieved from https://1ref.us/1cw, accessed 8/20/20.

[22]"Theology of Ordination Study Committee completes work (UPDATED)," June 5, 2014, available at https://1ref.us/1cx, accessed 8/20/20.

church office without conversion, (2) those who believe that LGBT persons can become members of the church and hold office while struggling with homosexual tendencies as long as they do not publicly commit homosexual acts, and (3) those who believe that homosexuality is mainly a genetic condition and, therefore, that the church should accept LGBT persons into membership and church office even if they do not alter their attitude and behavior.

The last category of Adventists mentioned above represents the most extreme of the progressives; they are inclined to accept gay pastors and same-sex marriages. On the other hand, there is also a minority of extreme Adventist conservatives who are inclined to totally ostracize LGBT persons and not offer any redemptive strategy to reach them.

Scripture is clear concerning God's displeasure of homosexual relations. Yet, as has been referenced above, several Protestant church denominations now embrace same sex-marriage and gay clergy. One of the candidates for president in the United States in the 2019–2020 election season, Mayor Pete Buttigieg, has claimed to be a person of faith and a follower of Scripture, yet he is brazenly married to another man. How can there be such confusion on an issue that is so crystal clear in the Bible?

If, in our lives, the Bible ranks as a lesser or equal authority to personal experience, science, ideology, religious affiliation, or family ties, then we are likely to have a distorted view of homosexuality and other issues. The Scriptures should be the most authoritative factor in our perspective of homosexuality. However, when believers view the Bible as merely one source of authority among others and they use methods of interpretations that allow them to construe certain passages of Scripture in ways that destroy the literal sense, they open the door for the adoption of erroneous beliefs and practices.

One distorted belief concerning homosexuality has been often expressed in the following manner: "Homosexuality is not worse than any other sin because all sins are equal in the sight of God." The notion that all sins are equal in the sight of God sounds plausible on the surface, but it is incorrect. The Bible does teach that all sin is offensive to God and that any sin can separate us from God, but it does not teach that all sin is of equal value or magnitude. There are certain sins that are more destructive to God's original order than others, and there are also certain sins that are more deleterious to the moral and spiritual well-being of individuals and communities than others. Our conscience and moral judgment suggest to us that all crimes are not on the same level. For example, a starving homeless person who steals a loaf of bread from a supermarket is not worthy of the same punishment as someone who murders another person in order to steal his wallet. The magnitude of the transgression is different, therefore, the punishment needs to be different.

Likewise, while all sexual sins have a habit-forming-pleasure-inducing mechanism, we can safely infer that, in God's moral judgment, homosexuality is of far greater magnitude than that of premarital sex and adultery. Pre-marital sex represents a consequential departure from God's will, yet it is not as severe as adultery, which often causes emotional, psychological, and spiritual damage to the entire family. Adultery, in some cases, leads to dissolution of the family. However, while premarital sex and adultery are sexual sins with different degrees of damage to one's personhood and one's family, these sexual sins do not, in effect, reverse God's creative order. Conversely, homosexual cohabitation turns God's creative order upside down. It moves beyond the scope of a habit-forming-pleasure-inducing sexual sin to that of uprooting God's original arrangement of how male and female were made to function. It also crosses the gender relation boundary that God established at Creation. One of the consequences of uprooting the perimeter around gender relations that God instituted at Creation is that it destroys the existential cornerstone of society. If the foundational building blocks of society are removed, the human species will collapse morally, spiritually, emotionally, and in every other way.

As we have mentioned, the Bible has some clear admonitions against engaging in homosexual cohabitation. For example, in Leviticus 18:22, God calls homosexual relations an "abomination." Notice the clarity and severity of God's commandment: "You shall not lie with a male as with a woman. It is an abomination." Scripture also refers to homosexual cohabitation as something that is "against nature." In other words, it is so perverted that those who engage in it have "changed the natural use" of what God designed sexual relations to be. Paul makes this point very forcefully in Romans 1:26, 27: "For this reason God gave them up to vile passions. For even their women exchanged the natural use for what is against nature. Likewise also the men, leaving the natural use of the woman, burned in their lust for one another, men with men committing what is shameful, and receiving in themselves the penalty of their error which was due."

The Scriptures also contain evidence that God's power can transform homosexuals into committed heterosexuals. Paul revealed in

1 Corinthians 6:9–11 that some of the current members of the church in Corinth had formerly been homosexuals but that they had been cleansed, justified, and transformed by Jesus Christ and the Holy Spirit. Paul's message is actually a message of hope for the LGBT community: it declares that transformation is possible through Jesus Christ and the Holy Spirit. It is this accessibility to divine transformation that nullifies any justification of homosexuality founded on the argument that some people have genetic tendencies toward homosexuality.

Although the preponderance of evidence indicates that homosexuality is a learned behavior, it is also probable that sin has impacted the genetic material of some human beings in such a manner that it has produced proclivities toward same sex cohabitation. Now, the fact that a person has a propensity toward a certain behavior does not excuse that behavior if such conduct is forbidden in Scripture or is hazardous to human beings. A person might have a genetic weakness toward the drinking of alcoholic beverages, yet this does not excuse the moral responsibility of a person if he or she chooses to get drunk, drive a car while intoxicated, and kill someone else. Drunkenness is still a sin for which that person will ultimately be held accountable by God. God will not condemn people merely because of their propensity; however, when people refuse to take advantage of the ultimate antidote to their addiction and the resources for their salvation that God has provided, then they will be condemned.

The fact that Jesus Christ and the Holy Spirit can transform people with same-sex tendencies is a clear indication of where the church should focus its energies and resources in ministering to the LGBT community.

Likewise, a person with strong tendencies toward same-sex cohabitation or any other weaknesses is not condemned for the existence of the propensity. Rather, the condemnation comes when such a person refuses to seek divine transformation and instead rationalizes his or her weaknesses. Jesus addressed this point in figurative language when He stated: "And this is the condemnation that the light has come into the world and men loved darkness rather than light because their deeds were evil" (John 3:19). Using the same metaphors as Jesus, we are not condemned because we were born in darkness; rather, we will be condemned if we refuse to embrace the light that has come into the world—Jesus Christ and his plan of salvation and restoration.

The fact that Jesus Christ and the Holy Spirit can transform people with same-sex tendencies is a clear indication of where the church should focus its energies and resources in ministering to the LGBT community. The church should seek to lovingly *redeem* the LGBT community not lovingly *affirm their weaknesses*.

It is also worth reiterating that prevention should be a major strategy for the Seventh-day Adventist Church in dealing with homosexuality. In a misguided attempt to achieve the noble goal of equality, there is now a momentum in society to blur the lines between the genders and promote a sort of genderless world. Gender and role distinctions in the family and in society are thus sacrificed on the altar of putative equality. However, God's Word is very clear that His people should maintain gender distinction even in the clothing that we wear: "A woman shall not wear anything that pertains to a man, nor shall a man put on a woman's garment, for all who do so are an abomination to the Lord your God." (Deut. 22:5).

Gender distinction is a preventive measure against homosexuality and the reversal of God's created order. Notice that, in Deuteronomy 22:5, God calls the failure to maintain gender distinction in clothing "an abomination." In ancient times, men did not wear pants, so this is not necessarily an injunction against women wearing pants. However, it is a clear command to wear clothes that distinguish between male and female. Trends in the fashion industry have made it increasingly difficult to find modest clothing that clearly maintains a line of demarcation between male and female. Nevertheless, if we are selective and vigilant, we can find such clothing in today's marketplace. Yet, notice again that the larger principle in God's command is that a lack of gender distinction and same-sex cohabitation are "an abomination" because they reverse God's created order; therefore, God's people must be vigilant in these areas.

There is no way that any of the passages of Scripture that I have referenced in regard to homosexuality can honestly be interpreted in a manner that supports homosexual relationships. However, as has been mentioned, some churches have either embraced or dabbled with hermeneutics that undermine the authority of Scripture. Consequently, they have found ways to force onto Scripture interpretations concerning same-sex relationships that are patently inconsistent with both the immediate and the general context of Scripture.

Abortion and the authority of Scripture

As with the topics of women's ordination and homosexuality, the Scriptures should be the final authority regarding abortion. The Bible is clear that God forbids premeditative murder, except in cases of self-defense or capital punishment. In Genesis 9:6, God said, "Whoever sheds man's blood, by man his blood shall be shed; for in the image of God He made man." In this passage of Scripture, the value of human life is linked to the fact that human beings were created in the image of God. A major question in the abortion debate should be whether or not the unborn baby is created in the image of God. In other words, at what point in its development is the fetus made in the image of God?

In our quest to answer these questions, we should consider the implications of several passages of Scripture that reveal that God takes special notice of the unborn fetus as if it has a value equivalent to a human being. First, notice that in Psalm 139:16, David emphasized that while he himself was yet unformed in the womb, God had a detailed biological blueprint concerning who he was designed to be: "Your eyes saw my substance, being yet unformed. And in your book they were all written, the days fashioned for me, when as yet there were none of them."

Second, Scripture shows that God set apart for His service several persons in the Bible during their prenatal stages. For example, in Jeremiah 1:5 God spoke the following words to the prophet, "Before I formed you in the womb I knew you; before you were born I sanctified you; I ordained you a prophet to the nations." The word "sanctify" means to set apart for a holy purpose. If God sanctified Jeremiah before he was born, then it implies that God considered Jeremiah's developing fetus to be of a value equal to the baby he would be when he would be born. According to Judges 13:5, Samson was to be "a Nazarite to God from the womb." The apostle Paul emphasized in Galatians 1:15, 16, "It pleased God, who separated me from my mother's womb and called me through His grace, to reveal His Son in me . . ." The angel Gabriel predicted in Luke 1:15 that John the Baptist was to be "filled with the Holy Spirit, even from his mother's womb." Furthermore, when Elizabeth was six months pregnant with John the Baptist, the unborn baby within her leaped with joy in the presence of the yet unborn Messiah in the womb of Mary (Luke 1:39–45).

Third, Exodus 21:22, 23 is especially germane to the question of whether or not God views the fetus as of equal value to the postnatal child. In these verses, God states the following:

> If men fight, and hurt a woman with child, so that she gives birth prematurely, yet no harm follows, he shall surely be punished accordingly as the woman's husband imposes on him; and he shall pay as the judges determine. But if any harm follows, then you shall give life for life. (Exod. 21:22, 23)

This passage of Scripture has been the object of much attention and scholarly study in the abortion debate. Dr. Ron du Preez has provided a succinct analysis of the scholarship applied to these verses in his perspicuous exegetical exposition in his book *Morals for Mortals*.[23] According to Exodus 21:22, if someone hurts a pregnant woman so that she gives birth prematurely, that person should be punished in accordance with that which the woman's husband deems to be fair compensation because, in spite of the hurt to the woman, the baby comes forth alive and well. However, if the unborn dies or is born prematurely and then dies or if the woman dies, then life is required for life. In other words, God places equal value on the life of the unborn or premature baby as on the life of the mother. The clear inference is that, because each is made in the image of God, the life of an unborn fetus or of a premature baby is of equal worth to the life of the mother.

Evidence from biology indicates a rapid development of the fetus. By the fourth month of pregnancy, the average fetus has all its limbs, and it can definitely feel pain. To interfere with such a rapid developmental process—the result of which is a unique human being made in the image of God—is to play God.

The vast numbers of abortions carried out do not involve extreme issues like the life of the child threatening the life of the mother—referred to as "therapeutic abortion." Rather, in most cases, they are "elective" abortions or abortion "on demand," in which the mother chooses to not let the fetus develop to the point of birth, thereby terminating the rewards and consequences of a new helpless human being. Sadly, many people seek to save their dogs and cats from harm and distress. Yet, for a variety of reasons, they are willing to subject unborn human beings to the pain and distress of abortion. Today, society seeks to minimize and obfuscate

---

[23]Ron du Preez, *Morals for Mortals* (Berrien Springs, MI: Omega Media, 2006), chap. 8.

the moral issues surrounding elective abortion by the use of euphemisms and inaccurate phrases such as "termination of pregnancy," "pro-choice," "a woman's right to choose," and "a woman's control over her own body." However, Scripture clearly indicates that the unborn fetus should be treated with the value and respect that we accord to human beings who have been born.

Summary

Amid a society that is reactively seeking to distance itself from the abuses of traditional thought and practice in both government and church, Seventh-day Adventist Christians are confronted with a variety of difficult contemporary issues such as women's ordination, homosexuality, and abortion. The authority of Scripture and proper hermeneutics are crucial for understanding these issues and making decisions that will meet God's approval.

Chapter 6

A Way Forward

The previous chapters have shown that Scripture reveals a paradigm of leadership in the church based on the appointment of men as spiritual overseers, particularly in the roles of apostles, elders, and deacons. Women were not appointed as apostles, elders, and deacons in either the Old or New Testaments, though they engaged in ministry and leadership in a variety of ways, such as a prophetess, a mother, or a care-taker/philanthropist. Also, on a few occasions, they served as assistants to male spiritual overseers. Therefore, while Scripture supports the involvement of women in a variety of ministry roles, it does not support the ordination of women as pastors, elders, or deaconesses.

The Seventh-day Adventist Church is confronted with the necessity of comparing its own dubious practice of ordaining women as elders but not as pastors with the consistent practice of Scripture in not ordaining women to the offices that constitute primary spiritual oversight. Although the Seventh-day Adventist denomination has never voted in a General Conference session to ordain women as pastors, it has endorsed the ordaining of women as elders and has also left the door open for women to become licensed pastors. As mentioned above, the current practice of the world church is both unscriptural and impractical. By ordaining women as elders without the consent of Scripture, the denomination encourages a desire in women to be ordained as pastors without the authorization of Scripture. Yet, when these women seek ordination as a pastor, they are told that they cannot be ordained due to a lack of biblical support. This is confusion! There is only one way to be faithful to the Word of God and to get out of the current confusion: that is, to prayerfully and courageously reverse the decision to ordain women as elders and to not encourage women to become pastors.

As difficult as such a decision might be, it will demonstrate faithfulness and consistency in adhering to the authority of Scripture. It will also stem the frustration and pain that many women go through as they have been ordained as an elder and given pastoral credentials yet are jilted from being ordained as a pastor. Again, the current practice of ordaining women as elders but not as pastors is tantamount to confusion. It also lacks compassion and foresight.

The predicament that the Seventh-day Adventist Church finds itself in with respect to women's ordination is analogous to the predicament that the chosen people found themselves in during the time of Ezra when many of the men of Judah and Israel, including several priests and Levites, had married nonbelieving wives from other nations in opposition to God's commands. According to the ninth and tenth chapters of Ezra, after Ezra, in astonishment, had rent his garments and plucked out some of his own hair and had fasted and prayed in shame and humiliation at the transgression of his people, a large assembly of men, women, and children gathered before Ezra. The leaders of the people then made a covenant with God to put away their nonbelieving wives. Though this decision would be extraordinarily painful and disruptive, Ezra and the leaders outlined a clear procedure to facilitate the faithful implementation of the oath to divorce pagan wives and to eschew non-missional fraternization with the heathen nations around Jerusalem. Accordingly, all the men who were guilty of this particular transgression followed through with their promise to divorce their pagan wives.

The marriage covenant is among the most sacred and pivotal contracts given to humanity. God declares, in Malachi 2:14–16, that He hates divorce—particularly because of the suffering that it brings upon the wife and, by extension, the family. Moreover, in 1 Corinthian 7:12–16, Paul recommends that new converts who are already married to an unbelieving spouse not divorce their spouse if the spouse choose to remain married. Thus, from our retrospective viewpoint, it would not have been unreasonable for the Jewish husband who was married to a pagan woman to repent of his past transgression against the Lord while still remaining married to his pagan wife, provided that she did not oppose her husband's religion.

We can imagine that there were some of God's chosen people in Ezra's time that viewed the decision to put away pagan wives as the most disruptive and insensitive thing that could be done. They quite possibly argued that it was more reasonable to keep the pagan wives than to divorce them and that the husbands would teach their children not to follow their own example in choosing a pagan spouse. Such a strategy would seem reasonable. However, Ezra and the leaders were well acquainted with the fact that Israel's intermarriage and non-missional fraternization with heathen nations led them away from God, which resulted in divine chastening for seventy years in Babylonian captivity. Ezra and the leaders did not want to repeat the painful lessons of the past, especially as they were reconstructing the holy city, the temple, and a new culture of faithfulness to God. The Bible implies that God accepted His penitent people's covenant to divorce their pagan wives in this particular situation.

The main idea of this particular story in the book of Ezra is that, although the reversal of a previous agreement can be very painful and disruptive, if a previous agreement puts us in conflict with God's revealed will, we should do our best, if at all possible, to reverse it. The painful task rests upon the leaders of the Seventh-day Adventist Church to reconstruct a new culture of faithfulness to God by showing that it is better to follow Scripture, even when it is inconvenient and disruptive to do so, than to maintain an unbiblical precedent. Some people will argue that to reverse the decision to ordain women as elders will precipitate a break away from the Seventh-day Adventist Church by the majority of those who are in favor of women's ordination. Such a reality is very probable. However, we should also be aware that the world church's current compromised position on women's ordination closely correlates with a downward spiral toward the embracing of other unscriptural ideologies and practices, such as the accommodationist approach toward homosexuality, abortion on demand, and a variety of worship styles that involve a mixture of the sacred and the profane.[24]

---

[24]See Michael G. Coleman, *Reflections on Issues in Music and Worship* (Fort Oglethorpe, GA: TEACH Services, Inc., 2019); Dave Fiedler, *Tremble* (Coldwater, MI: Remnant Publications, 2014); Stephen Bohr, *Worship at Satan's Throne* (Coldwater, MI: Remnant Publications, 2008).

As mentioned above, the Seventh-day Adventist Church is now in a predicament reminiscent of the Missouri Compromise. The untenable position of maintaining slavery in the South, abolition in the North, and tolerance of slavery in some mid-western states eventually led to secession and the Civil War. Our present compromise in ordaining women as elders but not as pastors will in time either lead to the secession of the pro-ordination constituents and the splintering of the Seventh-day Adventist denomination or to the entire denomination's embracing of women's ordination as a *fait accompli*. However, a courageous reversal of the policy of ordaining women as elders will demonstrate the church's commitment to the authority of Scripture, and such an action will likely motivate faithfulness to God in many other areas by the greater portion of the denomination, even if a contingent of the denomination were to break away.

The way forward is not smooth or easy. Rather it is narrow and painful. However, the future happiness of the Seventh-day Adventist Church is dependent on how faithfully our leaders adhere to the Word of God. If we, like the contrite leaders in the days of Ezra, make a covenant with God to unswervingly follow the Scriptures, the Seventh-day Adventist Church will surely reap blessings from the Lord that will follow us long after this generation of leaders has passed away.

www.ingramcontent.com/pod-product-compliance
Lightning Source LLC
Chambersburg PA
CBHW060442090426
42733CB00011B/2362